Let's Be Friends Series, Book 1

Stepping in the **Light**
Life in Joy and Power

Howard R. Macy

Friends
United Press
Richmond, Indiana • www.fum.org

Let's Be Friends Series, Book 1
Stepping in the Light: Life in Joy and Power

Copyright 2007 by Howard R. Macy

ISBN 0-944350-69-0
    978-0-944350-69-0

Articles written from 1979–2006 and reprinted by permission of
Quaker Life magazine, 101 Quaker Hill Drive, Richmond IN 47374.

Cover Design: Shari Pickett Veach

Friends United Press
101 Quaker Hill Drive
Richmond IN 47374
friendspress@fum.org
www.fum.org

Library of Congress Cataloging-in-Publication Data

Macy, Howard R.
  Stepping in the light : life in joy and power / Howard R. Macy.
    p. cm. -- (Let's be friends ; bk. 1)
  ISBN-13: 978-0-944350-69-0
  1. Christian life--Quaker authors. I. Title.
  BX7731.3.M33 2006
  248.4'896--dc22
                       2006029446

With gratitude to

Jim and Barbara Perkins

friends and encouragers

who helped open the way

Table of **Contents**

Introduction

By Howard R. Macy

"And we, with our unveiled faces reflecting like mirrors the
brightness of the Lord,
all grow brighter and brighter
as we are turned into the image that we reflect;
this is the work of the Lord who is Spirit."
(2 Corinthians 3:18, JB)

Children of Light. Publishers of Truth. The earliest Friends took these bold names to describe how their encounter with Christ transformed them. Many of us are challenged still by their compelling lives and witness (and of those who followed them), and we know that they require more than mere admiration or shrine-building. Instead, they invite us to listen deeply and to explore how we might best live today.

The essays collected here are occasional adventures, trying to discover how the time-tested witness of others might guide our ordinary living. They rise out of living, reading, friendship, pertinent and impertinent questions, trying to walk in the Light of Christ, and much more. I offer them to readers as we search out together living as Children of Light.

This book gathers columns that first appeared in *Quaker Life* from 1979 to 2006. At Jack Willcuts' invitation, which I still cherish, many of them were also published in the *Evangelical Friend*. I want to thank especially two editors of *Quaker Life*—Jack Kirk, who invited me to take a turn writing the column "Let's Be Friends," and Trish Edwards-Konic, who included me among the writers who have shared the columns "Bible Study" and "Soul Food." I am deeply grateful for their confidence and encouragement, not to mention patience. Of course, I'm eager to thank both of the readers who sent fan mail. They really egged me on.

These essays are personal reflections growing out of living and serving among Friends, not only in my teaching at Friends University and George Fox University, but through traveling in the ministry and learning from a widely scattered company of friends and colleagues. In *A Testament of Devotion* Thomas Kelly writes warmly of "The Blessed Community." As I have gathered and edited these essays, I have been reminded of how extravagantly God has blessed me in giving me such a community, an amazing company of colleagues, mentors and friends. I thank God and each of them.

Sometimes the essays will retain specifics of the persons or of the times and events that prompted them, but I think that such particularities will not detract from the larger message. In the end, I hope these essays will help us live thoughtfully and faithfully as followers of Christ, our Present Teacher.

Working with Trish Edwards-Konic and the staff of Friends United Press has been delightful. For help in gathering and preparing of these materials I especially want to thank Margaret Fuller, a gifted administrator in the Department of Religious Studies at George Fox University, and David Way, whose support work was timely and invaluable.

Foreword

By Jack Kirk

Across the years Howard Macy has spoken, lectured, preached and taught classes for North American Quaker groups from New England to Oregon. He has brought us a deeper awareness of the spiritual discoveries of the first generation of Friends and challenged us with fresh implications of what it means to apply them to our lives and world situations today. I have been with him when he has addressed and stirred Quakers in New York, California, Indiana and North Carolina. He knows intimately the Living Christ who spoke to George Fox and Margaret Fell and Thomas Kelly; his field of expertise is the Old Testament Scriptures, so he has moved amongst us as a modern-day Jeremiah or Isaiah calling us back to the One who first called us forth as a unique people of faith. If you have missed one of his messages, addresses or classes, you have missed a rich spiritual experience.

But if you have missed Howard Macy in person or wanted to spend more time with him or wished you could share his insights with your meeting—we now have this book. I have been touched in significant places as I have gone through the manuscript. It has been just like some warm, face-to-face visits with Howard in which he has shared some of his most deeply felt concerns for Friends. His humor and compassion, his sense of spiritual urgency and realistic hope come shining through. One completes the adventure through the text convinced that one is once again back in touch with the heartbeat of a vital Quaker Movement.

Howard communicates the wholeness of the original Quaker vision in these pages. He is able to speak to both programmed and unprogrammed meetings. He is aware of the dynamics of living Quaker spirituality and points us toward them. He has been a student of the characteristics of healthy Friends meetings and sets them forth. He understands clearly the intent for the creation of Quaker entities like Elders and Queries and Meetings for Clearness and calls us to embrace them fully. This is a great study book for a Ministry and Counsel or a Committee of Overseers. Sunday School and First Day School classes will find a treasure of rich material to mine and the Study Guide that follows is most helpful.

Years ago when I first became editor of *Quaker Life* magazine I wanted to carry a column in each issue that would paint a portrait of a renewed and dynamic Quaker Movement that could again speak to the condition of a weary, jaded and dark world with something of the fervor and passion of the first "Children of Light" (our name before we were called "Friends" or "Quakers"). I wanted the column to articulate practical steps that could enable us to move toward making the vision a reality. I was able to persuade Howard Macy, who was then a professor in the Religion Department at Friends University in Wichita, Kansas, to take on the duties of writing the "Let's Be Friends" column and my hopes were more than fulfilled. All of the articles in this book first appeared in the pages of *Quaker Life*. They are just as relevant when applied to the Quaker Movement and its calling in the world today as they were then. The principles of vital faith are the same in every age whether it was the first followers of Jesus, Francis of Assisi and Sister Claire and their band of brothers and sisters or George Fox and Margaret Fell and the Valiant Sixty, the daring young men and women who first took the Quaker message throughout Britain, Ireland, Scotland and Wales, Britain's North American colonies and then anywhere in the world that a British sailing ship would carry them.

The situation in the world today is very discouraging–wars, genocide, violence in the name of God, threats of worldwide plague, global warming, greed run rampant and polarization (no one listens to anyone any more). There is a thick darkness that can be felt. It is easy to be overwhelmed by it all and believe that no one person or group can make a difference. In the midst of this Howard Macy holds up the note of hope. It is not a shallow, sentimental hope, but hope based on what God has done, is doing and will continue to do in the future. George Fox saw a vast ocean of darkness and death in his own barbaric age. But, as Howard points out, Fox knew from his own experience that there was an infinite tide of God's light and love that sweeps over the sea of darkness. The light shines in the darkness and the darkness can never ever put it out. (John 1:9) We need this note of hope to have the courage to act with compassion in the present age.

My friend—Howard Macy—has written this book. The world is literally dying for lack of the Quaker way in action. If you want to get serious about practicing the Quaker way with joy and gusto in the current hour, read the life-giving words Howard sets before us in these pages.

Jack Kirk
Greensboro, North Carolina

Lives That **Speak**

Walking Cheerfully

"Did Quakers ever laugh?" The question side-swiped me. In class we had been reading together about the passion and courage of the Valiant Sixty and other early Friends. They were bold and determined, sometimes "in your face" in a very in-your-face culture. But humorless? Surely not. A lot of the Quakers I knew laughed; some of our best leaders were also our best storytellers. Of course, the Quaker Oats man is always grinning, but oatmeal can do that for you.

I also took refuge in George Fox urging Friends to "walk cheerfully over the world." I've amused myself imagining Friend George clowning in a red-leather nose or James Nayler doing stand-up comedy in Bristol. ("Did you hear about the Quaker who caught a thief in his house . . . ?" Not again. Tee-hee.) Quakers did laugh, I'd guess, but more importantly, they did "walk cheerfully"—willingly, gladly, joyously. And their walk and their message won people over. In Fox's words, they did "possess what they professed."

When I admire their winsomeness, I am often drawn to the New Testament's stirring images of Jesus' followers as an inviting people: shining like bright stars in the darkness (Philippians 2:15), children of light (Ephesians 5:8), people who are the aroma of Christ spreading everywhere (2 Corinthians 2:14–15), letters from Christ to the world (2 Corinthians 3:2–3).

Because such people get noticed, Peter advises, "Always be prepared to give the reason for the hope that you have." (1 Peter 3:15 NIV) People will ask because they notice a different quality of life, and Peter's letter throughout explains what such a life is like: hopeful, joyous, and carefree; loving and compassionate; full of integrity; rejecting malice, envy and slander, and, instead, pursuing peace; a life of genuine goodness, not contrived or self-righteous; a life of gentleness, respect, and humility.

It is a life that embodies the Christmas message of "good news of great joy for all the people." (Luke 2:106 NIV) Overwhelmed by love, it is a life that sets Jesus' followers apart as resident aliens in the world to be "holy," God's "chosen people." It's a daunting vision in some ways, but, in spite of its challenges, would we really want to settle for less?

Peter knows that such lives may also invite criticism and abuse. People may "think it strange" that Christians have abandoned carousing and debauchery. They may "heap abuse" on them and "speak maliciously" about them, perhaps even impose suffering on them. Even now there's no shortage of critics who describe Christians as grim and grumpy, two-faced, sober-sided, back-stabbing, double-talking hypocrites. (Whew!) Sadly, sometimes they're right, and Christians know that painful truth even more than their critics. From the earliest church, about which Paul commented that "many live as enemies of the cross of Christ" (Philippians 3:18 NIV), to our own time, we know that transformation is difficult, often requiring correction, patience and compassion. We know, too, that even short of bona fide wickedness, we can dim our lights by caving into culture or, being human, by simply being clumsy or stupid. (Dim bulbs?) Still lives that return blessing for insult, that respond in gentleness and respect, says Peter, both embarrass slanderers and eventually bring them to praise God.

Along with "walking cheerfully," Fox urges Friends to "be patterns, be examples . . . that your carriage and life may preach among all sorts of people, and to them." It would betray our humility, I'm sure, to imagine that people will catch the joyous message from our lives alone. There is a time for "answering," for sharing good news. Yet we should often ask ourselves how fully our individual lives and our life together are good news to those around us. Do they shine into the darkness of cynicism and despair? Are they inviting? Do their joy and hopefulness baffle people or even prompt them to ask why? Do they show the authenticity and freedom and vitality that people long for? Are they full of light, and light-heartedness, and maybe even laughter?

Joy to the world, the Lord is come!

Children of Light

My friend's recurring dream nearly spoiled him as a Quaker. Though the details have slipped my memory (not his), the central image is still clear. It is an image of my friend as a youth in an open, lonely place being approached by a small host of Quaker heavyweights, elders dour in face, grim in spirit, and full of judgment. They approach relentlessly, each closer step creating a prison of negativism that confined and frightened a spirit which longed for freedom and joy. Try as he might, he could not escape.

Though the dream may be uniquely my friend's, the image of Quakers as a dour, gray-grim people is not. Friends of yesteryear were, in many minds, a people who more often said "nay" than "yea" and, true to their word, meant it. Many Friends today are seen in the same way, as congenitally negative people who are tirelessly against the world and its ways, whether in personal morality or in international issues of war and peace.

What is embarrassing is that Quakers have sometimes matched this image. But in their winsome days if Friends stood against some things it was because they could call people with joy to a better way. Part of one of George Fox's letters reminds us of this positive witness:

> "Now Friends, who have denied the world's songs and
> singing, sing ye in the spirit, and with grace, making
> melody in your hearts to the Lord. And ye having denied
> the world's formal praying, pray ye always in the spirit,
> and watch in it. And ye having denied the world's giving
> of thanks, and their saying of grace and living out of it,
> do ye in everything give thanks to the Lord through Jesus
> Christ. And ye that have denied the world's praising God
> with their lips, whilst their hearts are afar off, do ye always
> praise the Lord night and day. And ye that have denied the
> world's fastings, and of the hanging down their heads like

a bulrush for a day, who smite with the fist of wickedness,
keep ye the fast of the Lord, that breaks the bond of
iniquity and lets the oppressed go free; that your health
may grow, and your Light may shine as the morning."
(Epistle 167)

Those who lived this counsel became a people radiant in joy
and power, a people whose positive life and witness drew others to
join them in their glorious new life. How apt that they should call
themselves Children of Light, for they exposed the darkness while
embodying its bright alternative.

The New Testament often uses the metaphor of light to talk about
the lives of those faithful to God. They are to let their lights shine
in a way that will cause people to praise God. (Matthew 5:16) They
are to expose the works of darkness by the brightness of complete
goodness, right living, and truth. (Ephesians 5:8–11) Through their
innocence and genuineness they are to shine in the world like bright
stars. (Philippians 2:15) Through the work of the Spirit they are to
grow ever brighter as they reflect the bright glory of the Lord. (2
Corinthians 3:18) This is brilliant, winsome living.

The first Children of Light did not win their way by glowering
gloomily at a darkened world. Nor will we. But radiance born of new
life and joy in Christ penetrates the darkness.

Shine on, Children of Light.

Reckless Abandon

Whatever happened to good old reckless abandon? Has uninhibited
devotion to God disappeared altogether?

Even to ask the question sounds judgmental, but it presents itself
over and over again. Too often persons who are answering Christ's

call to costly obedience come to me in frustration. They have looked about them seeking individuals and churches to help them in their new life, and they have been sharply disappointed. Where, indeed, is the reckless abandon that they have just discovered in their own lives? The meetings and churches seem so measured, so reasonable, so under control, so constrained, so business-as-usual. The lively spirit of devotion that is willing to risk anything for the sake of knowing God is hidden, if not absent.

Perhaps the risk-anything spirit smacks of fanaticism, but religious fanaticism has good precedent. Jesus himself was suspect. One time his relatives set out to take charge of him convinced he was out of his mind. (Mark 3:21) The early disciples and many Christians through the ages have risked reckless devotion to God, often at the cost of great suffering. The classic stories of Quaker heroes like George Fox, Mary Dyer, Edward Burrough, and Margaret Fell remind us that no small measure of godly fanaticism guided their lives. No vigorous spiritual movement lacks it.

The danger in recalling the stories of the heroes of faith is that with imagination one can taste (however slightly) the thrill without taking any risk. We indulge in reckless abandon by proxy. We react much like we would to a friend telling about his rollercoaster ride. Our eyes may widen in false fright and our stomachs may even give a small empathetic surge, but we take no risk. So in the life of faith we may marvel at the saints and martyrs and even vicariously join in their adventures, all the while steadfastly unwilling to lose our lives for Christ's sake.

Still the truth imbedded in these lives of dauntless devotion pierces us to the core. We, too, have heard the heavenly call and we hear it still as it echoes through the labyrinthine halls of our scattered spirits. In our wisest moments we know that we may answer in only one of two ways: the yes of total abandonment to God or the no of rejection and half-heartedness. Mild-mannered religiosity is no choice. Some, giving themselves wholly to God, discover a new life of joy and power.

Others turn sadly away, cherishing, like the rich young ruler, the one thing more precious to them than knowing God. The deep longings that God has planted in our hearts can be answered only with reckless abandon.

In "Hasten Unto God" Thomas Kelly writes:

> "Have you said, 'If I followed out my God-hunger absolutely, people would think me crazy, and I'd do harm, by my fanaticism, to the cause of religion'? For shame! How much religious zeal is killed by so-called 'common sense?' The Society of Friends in recent years has been choking itself with common sense and sobriety. Better to run the possible risk of fanaticism by complete dedication to God than to run the certain risk of being examined by a psychiatrist, as Fox was taken to a surgeon to have his excess blood drawn off, than to measure our lives by our mediocre fellows, and, achieving respectable security in religion, be satisfied if we strike average." (*The Eternal Promise*, p. 74–75)

Dare we be fanatic enough to deserve the name "Quaker?" Dare we abandon ourselves to God? Dare we not?

Quaker Mush

Hypocrisy has been overrated. It always damages God's work, of course, but it threatens the Church much less than simple blandness. Routine, powerless piety undercuts God's kingdom far more than hypocrisy ever could.

Many Friends have heard annual statistical reports about membership and attendance at meetings. The numbers suggest (again) that we are treading water or even sinking. That's not the whole story, of course. But the truth is that, by and large, Friends of all varieties are merely bland. There are many meetinghouses in which one can hear decently constructed sermons, listen to good music or bask in a peaceful silence. But there is little sense of the power of God.

Powerlessness is particularly tragic among a people whose first generation lived steadily in "the power of the Lord." Perhaps the most common phrase in George Fox's *Journal* is "the power of the Lord was over all." In his letters, he pointed others to the same experience. "In the power of the Lord God dwell and live," he charged. "Mind that which is pure in you, that ye may grow up in the power, out of the form." In the face of persecution, he could joyfully advise, "And though ye have not a foot of ground to stand upon, yet ye have the power of God to skip and leap in." Surely it is not mere coincidence that in the same year the Quaker sweep of England began Fox wrote to all Friends:

> "My little children in the Lord God Almighty, this is my joy, that ye be all ordered and guided by the mighty power of God, and know it in one another, and know the voice, and the sound of the words, and the power of them. For words without power destroy the simplicity, and bring up into a form, and out of the obedience of the Truth. And therefore walk in the power of the Truth, that the name of the Lord God may be glorified among you, and his renown may be seen in and among you, and all the world my be astonished, and the Lord admired in the ordering of his people." (Epistle 79)

That "all the world may be astonished" is akin to the charge against early Christians that they were "the people who have been turning the whole world upside down." (Acts 17:6 JB) The power of the Lord comes visibly to bring freedom, wholeness, and great joy. It draws people to obedience to God. It stirs God's enemies to resist it. And it certainly is not bland.

What is remarkable is that we see powerful movements of the Spirit such as the Church in Acts, the early Quakers, and others as unusual exceptions to the way things should be. The New Testament views them as normal. Lukewarmness, it says, is abnormal and completely intolerable (see, for example, Revelation 3:15–16). The people of God are to be channels of "the power of the Lord." That is what God intends.

If bland isn't normal, then why is there so much of it? One reason, undoubtedly, is that many of us have not, like Jesus' first disciples, waited expectantly in prayer for God to send the Spirit in power.

Another reason may be that we have tailored our vision of reality to the smallness of our spirits. Instead of letting the magnificence of God's love and power leave us completely undone, we reduce it to mere grandfatherly doting and magic for Moses. Many of us make Jesus Christ so remote from us that we cannot see him as the example and enabler of what we are called to become. Only a few seem to believe that Jesus was telling his disciples (then and now) the truth when he said they would do even greater works than he. (John 14:12) If "the power of the Lord" is to come upon us, we must see with our hearts that it can. We need clearer and bigger images of the Truth.

A friend of mine met a woman the other day who thought Quakers were a club and who asked if we use electricity and running water. How quaint! How much I would prefer that she be astonished at us because of the power of God! I, for one, am tired of Quaker mush. I think God is, too.

Let's live and dwell in the power of the Lord.

Sanctuary

Though meeting for worship had barely ended, conversation had already centered on life's daily routines. One man nearly fell into his routine vocabulary. A quick "I can't say it here" barely stopped a vulgar or profane word while his face betrayed a mixture of relief, embarrassment, and self-amusement. He was glad not to have said such words in the "sanctuary," assuming, I suppose, that coarse words offend God less if they are not uttered in sacred space.

The idea of sanctuary is very common. Most religious traditions, ancient to modern, sophisticated to simple, hold that some places and times are holier and have more effective power than others. The ancient Hebrews were eager to go to the Temple although they were excluded from its holiest rooms. Soldiers have often objected to killing on Christmas or other "holy" days. Johnny and Susie are repeatedly warned against rowdy play in "the sanctuary." Sacred space is not merely an antique notion.

Our experiences in some measure justify holding to special times and places, but we are the poorer for seeing sacred space and time too narrowly. Certainly we can rightly be grateful for meetinghouses and appointed hours for worship in which we have encountered God together. But we deceive ourselves if we think that God comes to us in those places and times alone.

With a rather foreboding view of the divine nearness, some proclaim that God is present in all times and places, but mostly as a cosmic spy. Since we are inescapably under God's scrutiny, we are told, we had better keep the commandments and pursue righteousness. Or else. This view cannot stand alone, of course, but the profound truth in it goes far beyond a churchy version of "making a list and checking it twice, trying to find out who's naughty and nice." God is indeed present with an active concern for justice, peace, and right living. To scoff at this is perilous.

Still there is a more welcome way of seeing all times and places as sacred. In fact, to establish a habit of being conscious of God's presence in each moment and circumstance can be utterly life-changing. It was to this habit that Brother Lawrence devoted himself at prayers and in the kitchen peeling potatoes. It was this that Frank Laubach sought with his "game of minutes" seeing how many minutes in each hour he could consciously think of God.

In a sense, one's whole life can become a sanctuary, a time and space wholly filled with God's presence. When through our devotion our spirits and our moments become transformed into rose windows, vaulted ceilings, flying buttresses, and altars to invite God's presence, a wonderful new way of living emerges. Simply the awareness of the God of unfailing love buoys us up into joy. Worship and prayer become natural and spontaneous. One's ears seem better tuned to God's leading in very particular circumstances. It enables a life of discipline and strength. More than ever before we can join with God in redemptive acts of healing, comforting, releasing, and helping others to come to know God for themselves.

The Quaker lives of joy and power that we admire grew out of such a keen awareness of the promise of God. When Friends denied holy days and seasons, it was not to demean them, but to lift up all of life as equally a place of God's life and power. The ordinary idea of sacred space and time, then as now, was much too small. We would do well to imitate them by letting our lives become sanctuaries as well.

Sacramental Breakdown

As I sat on the low brick wall waiting (and waiting) for the emergency road service to arrive, a teasing question entered my mind. "Wait until I get hold of Foster," I thought. "I'll ask, 'Richard, what in the world can be *sacramental* about having my car mysteriously stalled at the post office?'" Then the question turned serious.

What, indeed, could be "sacramental" in this moment? De Caussade's *The Sacrament of the Present Moment* along with Brother Lawrence and Quaker teaching about the Present Christ ganged up to remind me that no time is God-forsaken. But it's not always easy to experience that. Life doesn't seem sacramental when children develop selective deafness to parents' voices, when the sink stops up, when your fast-food sandwich tastes no better than its Styrofoam container, or when your work gets so boring that mere drudgery would be a welcome relief. How is God present in such ordinary, even bothersome, times?

Though I didn't grab a Port-a-Eucharist from the trunk or sprinkle the car with holy water, I began slowly to get an answer. "God really is here," I thought more matter-of-factly than religiously. "Things will be okay, somehow." Then a sense of gratitude slipped in—for the car (however stubborn), for friends who had already helped, for a grassy lawn to lie down on while I waited.

That moment was changed from frustration to praise, and it has continued to remind me of simple, but wonderful, facts. First, God is indeed present in all of our moments, often waiting to be acknowledged and received. We expect God to come in dramatic times, of course, in profound moments of wonder or in the difficult hours of tragedy. Yet we are apt to be completely unaware of the divine presence in what is to us routine, annoying, or trivial. Jesus told a story about some people who, when they were sent away in judgment, objected, "But when did we see you hungry, or thirsty, or a stranger?" They had missed Christ in the ordinary.

God does care about and understand the pleasures and the pratfalls of being human. The Christ who is now is always with us and was with us before, was just as vulnerable to interruptions, bumbling friends, and exhausting days as we are. He understands our moments, small and great, so that none is so trivial or obscure that it falls outside of his care.

God knows our needs and provides for them. In some way, though sometimes veiled, God will use and transform for our good the stalled cars and broken plumbing of our lives. The power of the Master of the Universe is tender power, turned gladly toward us to touch our lives with joy and wholeness.

Waiting because of a balky, old car may not seem very important. In a way, it is not. Neither are most telephone conversations, days at work, or small acts of kindness. Yet the fabric of our lives is woven steadily by the moments of our living. It is in the ordinary times of our lives that God meets us to wrap us round with love and to speak peace to our inner storms. In everyday moments we can be guided, we can hear and obey. In any moment we can joyfully praise God, until out of the threads of hearing and obeying, prayer and praise we weave a pattern of sacramental living.

I suppose we'll still burn the cookies, get flat tires, and have to attend committee meetings. But I hope I'll harrumph about it less and less. Instead let's all receive and rejoice in Christ who is among us in all the moment of our lives.

Molded by Scripture

A sure way to pick a theological fight is to discuss one's "view of Scripture." In the classic battles, those with a "high" view of Scripture bombard their opponents while those who hold a "low" view are sometimes known to fire back. (The medium-highs, knee-highs, and not-so-highs often seem to get lost somehow in training maneuvers or find reason for conscientious objection to this war.)

Friends have fought over the Scriptures, too, as we know poignantly from divisive periods in our history. Others have misunderstood us, and we have misunderstood ourselves.

The Friends principle at this point is simple and sound. While insisting on the unique value of the Bible, we have held that the

Inspirer is greater than the inspired writings and is still active. On the one hand, this becomes a wholesome check against an idolatry of the Book which diminishes our sensitivity to the Spirit's continuing work as our Teacher who leads into all truth. Yet at its best, this approach also encourages us to cherish and use the Scriptures as an invaluable guide for faith and life.

Although correct doctrine about the Bible may well be important, our view of Scripture matters far less than our use of Scripture. The Bible is for reading, not for fighting over. Perhaps the best of the Bible's statements about itself shows this very pragmatic concern. "All scripture is inspired by God and useful for refuting error, for guiding people's lives and teaching them to be upright. This is how someone who is dedicated to God becomes fully equipped and ready for any good work." (2 Timothy 3:16–17 JB) Rather than ask whether we are thinking rightly about the Bible we should ask whether we are allowing the Bible to shape our thinking.

Those who read George Fox's *Journal* and *Epistles* are unavoidably impressed with how deeply Fox is formed by the Scriptures and with how thoroughly his public ministry is penetrated by them. This hardly surprises us when we recall the many hours he spent with the Bible even during his early years of searching. He worried his relatives when instead of depending on the priests' teaching he would go into the orchards or fields with his Bible by himself. Yet out of this he had "great openings in the Scriptures."

Fox's example and the witness of holy men and women through the ages demonstrate the importance of the discipline of regularly reading and studying the Scriptures. Yet today, although the Bible is more accessible than ever to those who want to know it, the level of biblical illiteracy, even among those who profess to value Scripture highly, is shocking. It is increasingly obvious that few people give substantial time to knowing God's message through the Scriptures. This failure contributes significantly to superficiality and weakness in the Church.

To plead for renewed attention to daily disciplines of Bible study is not to set the Book above the Author. Some have fallen into that sort of bibliolatry, to be sure, but it is as unnecessary as it is mistaken. Indeed, we need to recognize that God has chosen to communicate to us clearly through the Scriptures and that we ignore them at our own peril. To read and learn to know them well is another way of presenting ourselves teachable before God.

We can approach becoming intimately acquainted with the Bible in a variety of ways. Simply reading large portions of Scripture at normal reading speed can broaden one's knowledge of the whole Bible and give a perspective sometimes lost while trying to wring meaning out of each word. The repeated reading of a single portion such as the Sermon on the Mount or a short letter like Ephesians provides yet another kind of insight. Some have been helped by choosing a passage and, as a part of their Bible study, reading it each day for a month. Systematic Bible study is yet another approach. Whether one chooses to investigate a book, a passage, a theme, a word or a person, careful study deepens understanding while it enhances other approaches to the Bible.

Meditation on Scripture is an approach particularly suited to our understanding of how God works through the Bible. In bringing a phrase or verse before God in meditation we trust the Spirit who first inspired those words to work through them to teach us now. A discipline akin to meditation is memorization of the Bible. As we are faithful in this we create a reservoir of biblical truth that the Spirit can use at any moment to guide us and to minister through us.

Whatever our approach may be, Friends at their best have always gratefully received and used the Scriptures as a gift from God. Let's come to know the Bible well.

Above All, Prayer

When people first encounter George Fox's writings, they are usually struck by several prominent personal qualities: painstaking integrity, cleverness, courage, hardiness, insight into truth, uncompromising devotion to God. What most impressed Fox's friend and colleague William Penn, however, was that Fox knew how to pray. In his preface to the *Journal,* after noting Fox's considerable gifts in discernment, teaching the Scriptures, and more, Penn wrote:

> "But above all he excelled in prayer. The inwardness and weight of his sprit, the reverence and solemnity of his address and behavior, and the fewness and fullness of his words, have often struck strangers with admiration, as they used to reach others with consolation. The most awful, living, reverent frame I ever felt or beheld, I must say, was his in prayer. And truly it was a testimony that he knew and lived nearer to the Lord than other men: for they that know him most will see most reason to approach him with reverence and fear." (Nickalls, *Journal,* p. xliv)

To identify prayer as the most noteworthy trait of this remarkable man may be surprising at first. Further reflection, though, shows that this is exactly what we should expect. Without such a notable life of prayer, we would never have heard of the lad from Leicestershire, of sermons from Firbank Fell, or of anything Quaker. Prayer is at the core of any life lived in God's power!

Prayer is necessary but widely neglected. Despite abundant talk about prayer, books about prayer, prayer chains, and other encouragements to pray, it is clear that many Christians do not make prayer their habit. Yet it is because we need it so much that Paul advised, "Pray constantly." (1 Thessalonians 5:17 RSV) Far too many people live in fear, frustration, guilt, and spiritual weakness simply because they do not pray.

Some people avoid prayer because they think that it is too difficult or that they don't know how. Prayer can be hard work and it can be learned, but at its root it is quite simple. Tidy thee's and thou's and a perfect understanding of how prayer works have almost nothing to do with effective prayer. We can bring our feelings and needs, our prayer and adoration to God simply and directly, just as we learn to listen simply to guidance and response. Effective prayer depends not on technique but on knowing God. Feelings of inadequacy should never keep us from prayer.

Others neglect prayer because they are not persuaded it is practical. They don't really believe that "prayer changes things." Yet it does! Prayer is intensely practical and should be used as much more than a religious safety net to catch us when relying on our own wisdom and strength fails us. In our personal lives prayer becomes a source for guidance and power. It also becomes a way of giving genuine help to others. To pray for one another in itself offers an embrace of strength and encouragement. Beyond that, however, through prayer we release the power of God to touch our lives and circumstances. I do not understand all the mysteries of why this should be true, but I know that prayer is more practical than anything else I do.

Prayer, then, can be simple and practical. Above all, it is the place of words and stillness in which we come to know God. How wonderful it would be if we, as spiritual heirs of George Fox, were known, above all, to excel in prayer.

Hearing Voices

Perhaps you've seen the shirt that admits, "I do everything the voices in my head tell me" or its variant, "I do everything the voices in my wife's head tell me." I haven't yet worn such a shirt when I teach my clinical psychology students. They worry enough already. But, oh, there are voices! You probably hear them, too.

Many of us hear the voices of the inner committee of selves that compete for our attention. When we're scattered, not centered, they can get loud and rowdy. The duty voice, family voice, civic voice, please-people voice, let-me-outta-here voice, and many others can whisper, yell, or nag us endlessly.

Then there are the outside voices, sometimes shrill, sometimes seductive, talking over each other to sway us. It could be radio, television, the papers, music, comedy, advertising, neighbors, people at work, little cliques of folk who trade bold judgments about topics they already know they agree about. All the voices together can create a cacophony that muddles and misleads us. The racket itself invites us to think about how to listen.

For me John Woolman's choice about listening is particularly compelling. He chose to order his life so that he could give "steady attention to the voice of the True Shepherd." Among other things, for him it meant changing jobs. For all of us, his choice points to the heart of simplicity: focus on the one Voice that can guide our listening and action.

Listening deeply to this Voice can help us see through the fraud, distortion, and self-interest that other voices often foist on us. Also, as we see in Woolman's example, such listening doesn't distance us from the world, but teaches us how to engage the world in strong, even surprising, ways. For Woolman it meant not only actively opposing slavery, but also reaching out to Indians, working to protect the poor, seeking the right use of animals, and more. For any of us such listening to the True Shepherd might guide us into still other ways of working for the healing of the world rather than merely worrying about it.

I've been worrying a lot lately, not that there's not plenty to worry about. But I catch myself a bit too eager to tune in to catch the latest bad news, especially hoping that it's bad for the liars and crooks who are messing things up. Maybe I could still get all the bad news I need by tuning in only half as often and using the rest of that time to listen more carefully to the True Shepherd. Then it wouldn't burden me to spend more time in proven ways of listening such as prayer, meditation, Bible-reading, and worship.

When we practice that choice it often sharpens our hearing for subtler calls, for the "nudges" that we hear more steadily in deeply centered living. Though God's voice can "shatter the cedars of Lebanon" or rattle rocky Mt. Sinai, it may come to us, as to Elijah, as a "still, small voice" or in the "sound of gentle stillness." It may be a simple nudge to make the call that turns out to be timely or do the simple act for someone that feels like grace to her. It may be to speak to someone, to send up a "flash" prayer, or to tell the boss you can't really keep lying to customers for him. A nudge might open our eyes to help one of the invisible people, which people at risk often are. The subtle voice may give us just the right words we need, as Jesus promised, or the wisdom just to be quiet.

Steady attention to the voice of the True Shepherd also lowers the other voices. Its tests them, puts them in perspective, even dismisses some of them. Over time, focused listening to the Voice makes that choice fuller and easier. It leads us ever closer to the day we could rightly choose to wear the shirt, "I do everything the Voice tells me."

The Tyranny of the Good

I don't remember any longer from whom I first heard the phrase "the tyranny of the good." It may well have been from my teacher, Elton Trueblood. I do recall, however, that many times since I first heard it I have fallen subject to such tyranny.

Almost daily "the good" makes its appeal for our energies to attend a committee meeting or a conference, to help a needy person, to give or listen to a talk, to send a contribution, or to respond to legitimate needs in dozens of other ways. It is precisely in the legitimacy of this multitude of appeals to us that temptation lies. After all, those who have any compassion or sense of justice or desire to serve God can hardly be unmoved by such calls. It is easy to say yes.

Yet we know it is folly to say yes. Soon the gentle good becomes a marauding horde laying siege to our lives. Our schedules become fragmented, our spirits shattered, and we leave untended the soil which allows us to grow—especially the soil of study, prayer, and worship. In the end, we are even diminished in our capacity to do the good.

The principal answer to the problem of "the tyranny of the good" lies in what is most likely to be ignored in helter-skelter living. It lies in submitting every choice and action to God's guidance, not in general but in very specific ways. It lies in standing still before God and waiting for orders.

The great Chinese Christian, Watchman Nee, raises the issue clearly through questions:

> "How much of the work you have done has been based on the clear command of the Lord? How much have you done because of His direct instructions? And how much have you done simply on the ground that the thing you did was a good thing to do? Let me tell you that nothing so damages the Lord's interests as a 'good thing.' 'Good things' are the greatest hindrance to the accomplishment of His will." (*Ministry to the House or to the Lord*)

In a similar vein, George Fox warns that whoever goes in service before being moved to do so by God becomes a "stumbling block . . . and is to be judged and condemned by the Light." (Epistle 33) Our good intentions can undercut God's good purposes. We should not expect that God will prosper any work however noble, which is not deeply rooted in the divine life.

So for the sake of our own lives and for the sake of the good, we must be patient enough and submitted enough to bring each choice before God. It is a patience well-rewarded, as Isaac Penington reminds us: "A few steps fetched in the life and power of God are much safer and sweeter than a hasty progress in the hasty forward spirit." (Leach, *The Inward Journey of Isaac Penington*, p. 30)

To live such a life in Christ requires daily, even momentary, resolve. It is possible. And we can help each other do it. I have friends who will inquire specifically whether I have sought guidance on a particular matter. That kind of accountability helps. We can help by encouraging each other to consider carefully specific opportunities for service instead of resorting to beg-and-pray arm-twisting to fill committee vacancies or Sunday school teaching positions. We can help by not burdening others with guilt if they do not feel led to take up actively the concerns which we care about deeply. It is better to encourage one another to faithfulness to God than to entrap one another into service that is not directed by God.

Meetings, too, need to consider whether each aspect of their common life arises out of fresh guidance from Lord. It is altogether too easy to fall into activity which arises from habit or tradition, on the one hand, or novelty, on the other. A meeting at all times should hold in its mind the question, "How much of the work which we do together is based on the clear command of the Lord?" Standing still before God and waiting for orders is necessary if we together are to know anything of the life and power of God.

How glad we can be because a vision of the good comes to us from so many quarters. Yet we can rejoice even more that we have an inward Teacher and Guide who can prevent the appeals of good from tyrannizing our living!

"Therefore all wait low in fear of the Lord, and be not hasty or rash, but see the way made clear; and as the Lord doth move you, so do." (George Fox, Epistle 83)

The Frantic Pace

Since summer often creates a change of pace after the intensity of spring schedules, it also gives rise to a flurry of resolutions. Tired folk everywhere promise themselves never to get so exhaustingly busy again. ("I've heard it before," complains the body. "But this time I mean it," replies the mind.)

Many long for order and a sensible pace in living to replace the frantic rush and scattering of energies that characterize their lives. Despite labor-saving devices and "fewer" working hours, the pace of life seems to accelerate rather than slacken. Even youngsters maintain such madcap schedules that they could well use daily appointment calendars. This way of living impinges on Friends lives together, but, more importantly, it diminishes the lives of those caught in its trap.

As an expert in frantic, I join those who yearn for a sense of order and peace. How we long for it. Yet how it eludes us! Sometimes we try to adjust the externals of our lives to ease our frustration only to discover that these are merely symptoms, not the cause of our chaos. Instead, scattered energies and shattered schedules arise at their root from a disheveled soul.

Noble rationalizations undercut honesty at this point. We prefer to tell ourselves, "It's important" or "Someone has to do God's work here" or "The experience would make me a better person." Such self-assurances, though justified at times, can easily hide the subtle self-centeredness that often produces feverishness.

The self can be pampered even through selfless work. The glory of praise for a job well-done and the vanity of being indispensable feed pride. Gluttony for activity and experiences satisfies self-indulgence. The inability to say "no" often shows how desperately we need the approval of others.

Those who do not know such selfish deceits can rejoice. The rest of us need to discover continually how single-minded devotion to God can transform bustling and burdensome lives into living that is buoyant and tranquil. Focusing and depending on God alone produces a radical shift which reorders life completely. That is why the greatest biblical command, to love God with one's whole being, is more wisdom than duty. It remakes life as it was intended to be.

In this single-mindedness, self indulgence is diminished by God's work within, pride weakens, and the tyrant need to meet others' expectations is defeated by knowing the loving acceptance of God. As we allow ourselves to be captured wholly by God, we are liberated to live in power and joy.

The busy rush of our lives can be curbed in some measure by techniques of time and personal management. But order rises from within. It is the order that comes from following our Guide, from not running ahead of our Light. When we can learn to heed God rather than our vanity or the polite coercion of others, then, as Whittier wrote, our ordered lives can confess the beauty of God's peace.

Let's rush only to God, there to discover the restful joy for which we long.

Life **Together**

Treasuring One Another

I'm feeling rich again these days, not because professors have suddenly been valued as much as professional football players, but because God has been teaching me anew to cherish my friends.

As I survey a potpourri of personal treasures, they call to mind the people behind them. The old table at which I am writing was Grandmother's, then Charlotte and Dorothy's. The watercolor of the fish market recalls the loving nurture of Wallen and Chris. The sofa and chair which once braved the indignities of Jack and Geraldine's children are now gradually being unsprung by my offspring. There's a dry fly from Wendell, a book from Hugh, an encouraging note once slipped under my windshield wiper, and much more, altogether a minor hoard of memorabilia which recall good friends.

These things that jog the memory are hardly a pirate's trove. Some, by ordinary standards, are probably even silly, but they are an irreplaceable treasure because they remind me of how rich I am in love. Almost everyone has a hoard of this sort. Each one has his or her own Jans, Wallys, Lauras, Dorothys, Marilyns, Jacks, and Kents. They are precious gems, none of whom we would trade for the wealth of the Rockefellers.

The treasure, of course, is not things, even though those of packrattish instincts might tuck mementos in odd or obvious places. Instead, the treasure is love shared, lessons taught, being believed in, being prayed for, laughing and crying together. It is the matchless gift of true friendship.

A playful cynic has coined the law, "Friends come and go, but enemies accumulate." My experience refutes him, but this is clearly a difficult time for friendship. Some have projected that loneliness will be one of the principal problems of the 1980s and among some, at least, friendships are abandoned easily in favor of pursuing wealth, status, or personal fulfillment. Mobility and many other societal pressures conspire to fracture meaningful relationships.

In the midst of these pressures we can learn both to rejoice in the friendships we have and to witness to how wonderful they can be. Though Christians have no absolute corner on friendship, one of the marks of the fellowship of faith at its best has always been a strong community bound together by love. Jesus expected it of his followers, and the earliest church displayed it in extraordinary ways. In the Quaker heritage, stories abound of persons who shared generously of their goods and offered up their liberty and even their lives in tender, unshakable loyalty to their friends. Such love is overwhelming to experience and winsome to all who see it. Who could fail to yearn for friendship like that?

The joy of friendship is both a treasure and a challenge. On the one hand, we should praise God for our friends. They are, after all, a remarkable gift, one that I am profoundly aware I do not merit. It is only right that we shower God with thanks for them.

On the other hand, love that has been so freely given reminds us to be more faithful in friendship ourselves. We should be eager to be kind, generous, patient, and self-giving, all of this without pretense, especially in the community of faith. This is part of our duty and our witness, to be sure, but it also brings great joy. It is for the sake of others and for our own delight that we have been commanded to love.

Let's cherish one another. Let's be Friends.

In the Care of the Meeting

In instant-replay analyses of the decade of the seventies, several commentators have pointed out its selfishness. Christopher Lasch in his book, *The Culture of Narcissism*, persuasively describes contemporary American culture as self-seeking. Motivated by desires for self-fulfillment, self-realization, self-discovery and other self-satisfaction,

Americans have clamored to be analyzed, encountered, and fulfilled, have devoured books on how to take care of "Number One," and in almost every conceivable way have pampered their "selves."

This contagious self-centeredness has also infected the Church. For example, it is not uncommon to hear people complain that they "don't get anything out of" various church programs or that they wished the church would "do something for me" or, only a bit less unselfishly, "for my kids." Though the church should nurture and encourage individuals, such complaints often have a decidedly self-centered tone. The church does not exist fundamentally to dispense personal happiness to those who honor the church with their presence.

Another expression of self-centeredness in the lives of churches and meetings is an unguarded insistence that each Friend should be completely free to follow his or her "own light." This is not only theoretically wrong in making each individual the absolute judge of what is true, but it also produces an anarchy which belies Truth and compromises our witness to the world.

Because the call to selfishness is so pervasive and so subtly persuasive in our time, Friends need to commit themselves anew to building the community of faith.

Christ's teaching clearly directs his followers away from selfishness and toward mutual concern and servanthood. Jesus' "new commandment" was that his disciples should love one another. Indeed, this mutual love was to be the identifying mark of the new Christian community.

The earliest Church took Jesus seriously as Christians committed themselves to one another not only in the life of the Spirit but also economically. This led later to the great teachings in the Epistles emphasizing oneness and mutual concern in the Christian fellowship. Give way to one another in obedience to Christ. (Ephesians 5:21) "Teach each other, and advise each other, in all wisdom." (Colossians 3:16 JB) Each of us should think of our neighbors and help them to become stronger Christians. (Romans 15:2) Such teaching throughout the New Testament clearly opposes self-centeredness of any sort in the life of obedience.

Our Friends heritage has, for the most part, also encouraged this community concern. When joining Friends, individuals put themselves "in the care of the meeting." Friends together are to "watch over one another for good." The extent to which we now retreat from such ideas may reveal how infected we are by modern self-centeredness.

Building the community of faith is very practical. As individuals, to commit ourselves to the community of faith is a continuing witness to the fact that we are not self-sufficient. To deny self-sufficiency is to admit our humanness. It is the first act of faith, an act perpetually renewed in committing ourselves to other Christians.

Not only is faith renewed, but in the give-and-take of mutual support, encouragement, teaching, and correction Christians also mature in faith and in their ability to serve in the Church and in the world. Tremendous energy is released when the faithful dedicate themselves to each other's growth and success.

The effect of this growth, however, can hardly be confined to the Christian community itself. Individuals mature to live more Christianly wherever they may be, and the community itself discovers ways to serve in the world together that no individual alone could sustain.

Though American self-centeredness may continue, Christ's call still challenges us. What a remarkable decade the 1980s would be if Friends were consciously to deny self-centeredness and were to commit themselves to one another in the love of Christ.

Instead of Hating Weddings

"I hate weddings," the visitor barked as she whisked out the door. "After they get married, they never like each other any more."

If we disagree with such a sweeping judgment, we can understand it. The disastrous state of marriage in American society casts the shadow of a question mark over almost every wedding. Even with the best intentions of both bride and groom, observers often wonder inwardly how long the marriage will last.

Especially in the last decade, the Church has focused great energy on the family. Various Friends meetings and institutions, for example, have sponsored seminars and retreats, held classes, shown films, provided counseling, and more—all to strengthen the family. This has often been helpful. Nevertheless, we might increase our effectiveness if we were more careful about the beginnings of marriages. An older Quaker custom may point the way for contemporary practice.

In earlier times, Friends meetings provided significant guidance for their members who planned to be married. The meeting, having been informed by the prospective couple of their intent to marry, appointed a committee to consult with them and their families and friends. Part of the committee's task was to consider after conversation with the couple and with others whether they were ready for marriage or whether there were barriers that commended postponing or even abandoning plans for this marriage. The committee also guided the couple as they prepared for marriage so they would have the most advantageous beginning possible.

Marriage "under the care of the meeting" was a good custom, though sometimes abused. Yet, by and large, it has fallen into disuse among modern Friends, probably for several reasons.

An obvious reason is that many couples are unwilling to submit genuinely to the guidance of others. Numbed by the assumptions of our culture and by the ethers of romantic love, they falsely believe that their marriage is strictly a private matter. It is not. Ultimately the unwillingness to receive guidance, before and after marriage, rises from common roots—pride and fear. The sooner these are set aside, the better the marriage will be.

Another factor in weakening the meeting's role in preparing couples for marriage is that many Friends have relegated this duty entirely to a pastor or other professional. This may be a way of deferring to someone with special skills in this area. It may also be a tacit recognition of the meeting's inability to help effectively. Sometimes Friends don't know how to help. At other times they simply don't have enough courage born of love to discourage a star-struck couple racing toward a foolish marriage, so would rather not take the chance of getting involved.

As much as possible, meetings need to discover creative, responsible ways of helping marriages before they are solemnized. Perhaps the following suggestions can contribute to the careful thought we must give to our ministry in this area.

- Educate young people more effectively about the meaning of marriage before they are seriously considering it for themselves. In addition to direct instruction, young people need to have close contact with strong marriages and families that can become memorable models for their future.

- Provide materials for couples anticipating marriage that will guide them in their planning and reflection. This could be done in several ways, including use of the meeting library and gift packets of materials for the couple to keep and use. Identify persons in the meeting who are particularly concerned and suited for this kind of ministry. Assist them to grow in their skills and sensitivity, so that in a spirit of love, they may become effective guides for the marriage-bound. In any meeting there should probably be several persons who could help in this way.

- Establish a process for counsel that those contemplating marriage are encouraged to follow. Surely this can be done lovingly and without legalism.

- Diminish as much as possible the giddy rush of excitement and the ostentatiousness often associated with the wedding ceremony itself. Instead, emphasize the seriousness of the commitments being made and the joy of worshiping God, who originated and prospers the glorious gift of marriage.

Rather than resigning ourselves to our society's cynicism and discouragement about weddings, let us, in every way we can, help marriages begin right.

On Being Noticeably Good

Undiluted goodness has suffered a great setback in popularity in recent years. In an age when our heroes are surrounded by compromise, deceit, and sexual innuendo, the desire to be noticeably good continues to diminish. As in all times, some people care nothing for right living. Many others, religious or not, aspire to be respectable, but not unusually good. But it seems that few devote themselves to living in a way that will capture attention and cause people to praise God because of their good lives.

We can understand the reluctance to be noticeably good. Very few persons want to be thought of as a "goody two-shoes." Almost everyone has encountered persons who tried to be good in ways that were merely obnoxious. (Perhaps such behavior is spawned in pride and insensitivity more than in righteousness.) Yet, even in face of our fears and of the current pressure toward mediocrity, Christian persons are called toward genuine, righteous living.

The New Testament makes clear to us that faithfulness requires lives that are tellingly good. They must be extraordinary. Jesus said, "You, therefore must be perfect, as your heavenly Father is perfect." (Matthew 5:48 RSV) However one may interpret this instruction, the high standard cannot be diminished. The church at Philippi was told, avoid anything in your everyday lives that would be unworthy of the gospel of Christ. (Philippians 1:27) George Fox and the early Quakers, who first called themselves Children of Light, were guided by this counsel to the Ephesians: "You were once darkness, but now you are light in the Lord. Live as children of light, for the effects of the light consists in complete goodness and right living and truth." (Ephesians 5:8–9 NIV) There can be no shadowy goodness for the Children of Light.

Though the command of the Gospel obligates us, its promise of a renewed life should also attract us. Like a beacon its hope pierces the darkness of our self-disgust and repeated failures. The Good News is that God through Christ can overcome our sin and can remake us. We can become what our most persistent hopes tell us we were intended to be.

We need to help each other toward that new freedom. Yet we may dim the vision of true righteousness by complacently accepting ordinary goodness. We may hold each other back by making silent pacts of mediocrity. We can fail by example and word to call out the best in one another. We can fail to encourage and to discipline one another—"to watch over one another for good."

Thomas Kelly warns us poignantly: "I believe *many* young people of tender vision and fresh sense of lofty, holy claims of God upon their lives are shocked by some of us who have good reputations but who have adjusted ourselves to conventional ways, and lowered our standards of dedication to God, and are stained with the mud of mediocrity." (*The Eternal Promise*, p. 27)

Conventional goodness is not worthy of the Gospel. It is too weak. It is living in forms rather than in power. In contrast, the Spirit of God, as we heed it, will guide us up to God and "thunder down all deceit within and without." A life renewed in power satisfies our deepest needs and witnesses to God's power in the world.

From the beginning Friends have cherished this extraordinary living. George Fox wrote to Friends in 1661:

"So that is the word of God to you all Friends, of whatsoever calling ye be; live in the power of Truth, and wisdom of God, to answer that just principle of God in all people upon the earth. So, let your lives preach, let your light shine, that your works may be seen, that your Father may be glorified. This hath the praise of God, and they who do so come to answer that which God requires, to love mercy, do justly, and to walk humbly with God." (Epistle 200)

The Timid Sixty

It took nerve for anyone to climb into the wrestling ring with the swaggering champion. But Edward Burrough acted even more boldly by seizing the ring in order to preach about wrestling against the principalities, powers and spiritual wickedness. Burrough was undaunted, just as he was when he calmed jeering, contentious crowds with his authoritative preaching during the "threshing meetings" at London's Bull and Mouth meetinghouse. Nothing but his untimely death in prison could stop young Edward Burrough.

Though Burrough's story is remarkable, it is not unique. So many of his Friends colleagues were actively proclaiming Truth over 350 years ago that they are known for convenience sake as the Valiant Sixty. In 1655, Francis Howgill worked with Burrough in London and Ireland. James Naylor preached in London. John Camm served in Bristol. Mary Fisher pioneered in the Barbados and suffered in Boston. Elizabeth Hooton, George Fox, William Dewsbury, and many others in many places preached about a Christ who was powerfully present in their lives of faith. The vigor and courage of the Valiant Sixty still amaze us.

We admire such a group of men and women, of course, but

preferably at a distance. Many Friends today would not welcome a Valiant Sixty. A Timid Sixty would be more quickly embraced as Quakers than their courageous counterparts. The temptation to prefer timidity to valor may arise from several misunderstandings. Some Friends, for example, seem to despair of having a sure message to proclaim. To reject simplistic creedal statements as insufficient and to seek to grow in understanding are important, of course. However, for "seekers" to proclaim the bad news of perpetual uncertainty completely contradicts the good news that the Valiant Sixty knew for sure about a Christ who is present to teach, guide and empower.

In the pluralistic religious atmosphere of our time, other misunderstandings arise. Some have come to think of truth in religion as mostly a matter of aesthetics. Much as one has tastes in music and food, so one may prefer to be religious or irreligious. Or one may choose almost whimsically what set of ideas will become one's private truth. Further, many regard it as impolite, certainly uncharitable, or even judgmental to suggest that a person's private truth might be wrong. The devilish error of our truth-by-whim age is to say, in effect, that truth doesn't matter.

Others think that their behavior is either good enough or bad enough to join the Timid Sixty. Some assume that their lives will reveal Christ without any words at all. Certain lives are almost that good, but those who lead them rarely think so. Many fear instead the possibility that their lives will belie the gospel. Some do. Nonetheless, personal perfection is not a prerequisite for sharing what is possible in Christ. Humility is fine. Hoarding the gospel is not.

Perhaps the "threshing meeting" would fail today. New times often require new forms. The task of proclamation, however, endures. Uncertainty must yield to confidence and timidity must defer to courage so that Christ may be known and Truth may prosper. "For God did not give us a spirit of timidity but a spirit of power and love and self-control. Do not be ashamed then of testifying to our Lord." (2 Timothy 1:7–8a RSV)

Convinced and Convincing

"Convinced" Friends are troublesome. Even when Quakers carefully avoid talking about their faith to anyone but other Quakers, some curious folk learn about the Friends message and are persuaded by it. Then they cause trouble.

Many convinced Friends, for example, know even better than "birthright" Friends what our distinctive message is and what Quakers should be like. And they care about it. After all, they have chosen this way freely. With their newborn enthusiasm and urgency, however, they can unwittingly create a disturbance. Old-timers don't like smart newcomers, so are apt to mumble unpersuasively about needing to understand "the Quaker way."

Another problem convinced Friends create frustrates them and embarrasses the rest of us. Their idealism too often meets a disappointing reality. In a sense they take an informational, driver's-license-type photograph of Friends and then show it to us. Without benefit of revealing only the best side and of retouching, we hope for grace since the photo probably does us justice. Friends' lives, we sadly admit, are often not as convincing as their message.

The caricature just drawn, like any other, is not entirely fair. Convinced Friends are neither always right nor perfect. Friends' lives generally are not a mockery of professed ideals. Yet there is a tension that reminds us that Quakers need to be both convinced and convincing.

All Quakers should be convinced Friends, understanding and believing the essential Quaker message. Without this, meetings stagnate and weaken while individuals are less able to live and share their faith effectively.

Even with occasional, brief classes about Quakers, far too little is being done to help people understand what they believe and why. Quaker students often remark to me with disappointment about how little they have been taught in their local meetings about Friends.

Where there is such negligence in training many important insights soon lose their meaning and become powerless traditions. In worship, for example, expectant waiting for Christ's teaching becomes two minutes (time it!) of ritual silence. Seeking the "mind of Christ" in meeting for business becomes mere "consensus." Emphasizing Christ's constant presence and the sacramental character of all of living becomes a hollow denial: "We don't observe communion." Without adequate instruction we can reap only a harvest of superficiality.

To insist that all Quakers be convinced does not plead for tradition for its own sake. It seeks instead to give identity to and to nurture modern Friends in their lives together and in the world.

Equally important, however, is that all Quakers should be convincing. People have a right to expect that our lives should match our words. Jesus advised his disciples to identify people by the fruit of their lives. The Letter of James agrees by insisting that one's actions should demonstrate one's faith. Though our lives can hardly be our only witness, they certainly must be convincing.

In conversation with an Irish Catholic tour guide during a trip to Ireland, it was challenging to hear her tell of the high esteem in which Irish Friends are held. She talked of Friends industrialists' unusual concern for their employees, of relief work at the time of the nineteenth century potato famines and of Friends concern for Irish Catholics when they were under persecution. In fact, during those persecutions, she said, "the Quakers were the only ones who were true Christians."

Many stories could be added which would illustrate a rich heritage of faithful living. The Quaker reputation is not unearned. What is important however, is that Quaker lives be as convincing now as they were then.

When thirteen-year-old William Penn first heard Friend Thomas Loe preach at Macroom Castle, he was very moved and wondered, "What if we could all be Quakers?" I wonder, "What if all Quakers were truly Quakers?" How convincing do you think we could be?

Ordinary People

The restaurant could have been switched with any of several hundred others in the Midwest and few would have noticed. The swarm of trucks outside reassured me that the food would be tolerable and maybe even good.

Inside, the spotted beige tile floor patiently masked most of the indignities it had suffered that evening. As I slid onto a chrome-and-vinyl stool and burned my tongue on my first cup of coffee, it seemed certain that I had been here before. Hadn't I seen that cash register—chipped beige paint held in place by a collection of yellowing notices curling back on themselves, defying the brittle scotch tape to hold them there? From the Dentyne in the candy case to the vinyl booths and Formica tables, it all seemed strikingly typical.

If the restaurant was typical, so was its late-night clientele. The waitress in Nikes, overfilled blue jeans and graying uniform top. The truck drivers with big buckles on dirty belts. The farmers with their Gro-More Feed caps positioned agriculturally on their heads. The cooks with jet black hair stacked and lacquered high above the jeweled corners of their glasses' frames. A man who looked as if he might be the local insurance agent. These people with others could have been the ten o'clock customers in the restaurant in anyone's town.

The place was unusually ordinary, but that is what caught my attention. It turned my mind to the ordinary folk of northwest England more than 300 years ago that became the core of the Friends movement. Mary Fisher may not have differed greatly from the young waitress. James Nayler could well have been much like the farmer in his cap. Indeed, almost all of the early Quaker preachers and missionaries were very ordinary—farmers, artisans, shopkeepers, hired hands, servants. The memorable fact about that ordinary band was that God's power through them challenged and shaped their world.

The thought that our early Quaker heroes were no more unusual than the folk surrounding me in the café brought me up short. I wondered—and have often wondered since—whether I can believe that the cluster of ordinary folk in that restaurant could be at the heart of a spiritual revolution. Or whether God can work powerfully in the world through a motley crew in Wichita. Or in Deep River, Fresno, Allen's Neck, Bend or Maple Run.

My mind is quickly satisfied about this. God seems to delight in working through ordinary people to do extraordinary things. After all, the Hebrews were mere slaves, Jesus was a common artisan, and his unlikely band of followers were mostly working Galileans whose distinct accent called into question their respectability the moment they opened their mouths. Paul reminds the Christians in Corinth, those whom the world thinks are common and contemptible are the ones God has chosen. (1 Corinthians 1:27–29) That has been God's way all along.

If I can persuade my intellect, however, it is harder to convince my heart. On the one hand I shrink from the spiritual cheerleaders who (often quite sincerely) try to coerce God into pouring out unusual power in their specific circumstances. That is too often the way to delusion and self-aggrandizement. Yet I am eager to receive whatever measure of grace God chooses to give. We can't force God's power to come, but we can prevent it from coming if we are not open.

Can I believe that ordinary people can do God's extraordinary work today? With God's help I think I can say, "Yes." Can you?

The Healing Light

A few weeks ago, now as I write, Agnes Sanford, a remarkable servant of God, passed away (1982). She is widely known for her teaching about healing and especially for her book, *The Healing Light*. What surprised me was to learn that this book came about because of an experience she had among Friends.

As she recounted the story, on one occasion Agnes was deeply impressed as she visited among Friends during a particularly powerful meeting for worship. At the conclusion of the meeting she asked, "What are you going to do with this?"

"With what?" Friends responded.

"With the presence—the power that heals. I'm speaking of the presence of the Holy Spirit. It's here. The place is full of its power. What do you do with it?"

Taken back, Friends replied tentatively, "We just enjoy it."

"That's not what it's for," Agnes urged. "It's to do the works of Christ."

Out of that experience, Friends invited her to teach them about the power that heals. *The Healing Light* grew out of her lectures to them. Since then, her insights into God's love and power to heal have helped many people.

There have been times, at least, when Friends clearly have known and used the powerful presence of the Spirit to do the works of Christ, including healing. The once lost *Book of Miracles*, for example, recounted stories about George Fox healing a variety of people and conditions. Fox's *Journal* contains some brief stories of this sort, most often about cases the physicians had considered hopeless. Perhaps the most intriguing is the story about a traveling companion of Fox who suffered a broken neck when thrown from his horse. Fox and the others took him for dead. Yet God's power through Fox's compassion (and head-twisting that would make even a chiropractor blush) revived him and restored his health. (Nickalls, *Journal*, pp. 631–2)

No doubt there are stories of healing among Friends in many of the generations between George Fox and today, but I don't know them. Nonetheless I do know a number of Friends who have quietly gone about this work of Christ in our time. I have heard testimony and stories of healing, simple to dramatic, which witness powerfully to God's love and active presence among us. Healing is not merely an ancient phenomenon.

Unfortunately, many Friends have been skittish about this topic. Healing has too often been viewed as a carnival sideshow featuring disreputable religious hucksters. On occasion it has been just that. The important thing to see is that the bright-lights-and-banners approach is not the whole story.

The simple truth is that the whole Gospel includes healing—new sight for the blind, leaping for the lame, hearing for the deaf, and more. It is an act of God's power and love through people who are compassionate and open to the life of God. It is a normal part of what it means to do Christ's work in the world. Even though healing has been misunderstood and abused, it is still a wonderful part of God's Good News.

Agnes Sanford's charge to Friends still seems fresh. The powerful Presence that we can know is not merely to enjoy, but to do the works of Christ.

Deadheads and Fanatics

Many think that Friends don't quake like they used to. What quaking there is, furthermore, may best be described as small tremors. Of course, Friends use a variety of quake meters, so differing interpretations abound.

A more difficult problem yet is that Friends don't agree on whether or not they should quake or on what quaking is. This issue has become divisive enough in several yearly meetings that it should capture our concern.

Some equate quaking with the contemporary Christian fascination with dramatic evidences of God's presence. They cherish flashy signs of lively personal faith. This "exciting" faith is sustained by prophecies, miracles small and great, the naming and numbering of one's spiritual gifts, "tongues" (sometimes), annual pilgrimages to religious enthusiasm festivals, and more. Some of this, in my judgment, is genuine and helpful. However, at other times it degenerates into a goose-bump religion promulgated by besequined musical saints and media gurus.

Christian faith can spawn genuine enthusiasm. Indeed, we expect that lives touched by God's life will show some signs of radiance. But the demand for "exciting" religion may unwittingly play to the spirit of our times—times in which boredom, fear, and meaninglessness have driven helpless people to the counterfeit satisfactions of emotional thrills, too often wholly contrived. Quaking and bouncing about with a grin may not be the same thing.

Other Friends observe such activities with a gray scowl. They shrink from signs, hide George Fox's *Book of Miracles*, and even question the reality or the depth of a faith that demands such high drama. Some are genuinely shy of hand-clappin', foot-stompin', "get-all-excited," old-time religion and would rather slip into the bleachers than take box seats in the "Amen Corner." If we can honor such natural reticence, however, we still should vigorously examine restraint.

In some quarters Friends maintain a wild excess of restraint. Some are so restrained, in fact, that they call to mind this notice seen in the local county courthouse: "The management regrets that it has come to their attention that employees dying on the job are failing to fall down. This practice must stop as it becomes impossible to distinguish between death and the natural movement of the staff." (Here we see the reason why meetings on occasion must be "laid down.")

Some restraint may rise from deep spiritual roots. On the other hand, it may be the fruit of pride, of uncertainty in faith, or even of barrenness of soul. It may betray a misplaced sense of religious etiquette. This, too, may play to our culture. In the face of religious pluralism and relativism, studied uncertainty is acceptable and sophisticated. Clear commitment and religious enthusiasm are not.

These two caricatures should remind us that we too readily judge each other as fanatics or deadheads. In doing so, we miss the point.

The essential question is not "How exciting is it?" or "How silent is it?" or "How traditional is it?" We must ask instead, "Is there genuine life?"

The expression of Christ's life within may be quite different in various individuals and meetings. This results in part from the personality and predisposition of persons and from God's choice to work creatively and uniquely in each person who will trust the divine purpose.

I have often marveled at George Fox's ability to take people to Christ their Teacher and "leave them there." I wonder whether we can't have enough tenderness to trust Christ's work in each other even while we encourage one another to greater faithfulness. Can't we have the integrity and the wisdom to explore our own spirits continually to discover the life of God seeking us, shaping us, and shaking us? Then, at least within our deepest selves, we'll quake.

Elders as Movers and Shakers (or Is That Quakers?)

To think of elders as movers and shakers throws the mind off balance for just a moment. After all, aren't elders the rock-solid guardians of the status quo (or, more pleasingly put, "tradition")? Sometimes. Most elders, however, can discern between growing while nurtured by the roots of tradition and keeping a root cellar. Even with that insight to their credit, elders are often thought to be backing slowly into the future (a position, by the way, guaranteed to cause a fall).

Suppose elders were pioneers. Suppose they were the cutting edge of a Friends meeting. If the elders are truly the leaders in Friends meetings, they should not be the dams that block the flow of new life. Instead, they should be the channels through which new life can surge. The best elders, in a sense, leave the fortress and scout the frontier. What would this be like?

Suppose, for example, that the elders were the first to carefully analyze the needs of the community that their meeting serves. And what if they were the ones actively proposing and supporting innovative ministries to meet those needs—whether through day care, peace education, Meals-on-Wheels, children's club programs, holistic health care centers or many other avenues?

Suppose the elders would take an active concern for the life of worship. They could assess together (continually, not annually) what actions or changes would enhance the openness, the depth, and the sustaining power of the meeting for worship. They could in many circumstances take a more active role in the life of worship. Whatever the pattern of worship, the elders' regular reflection on the life of worship would surely strengthen it immensely.

In a similar vein, suppose the elders were actively calling forth gifts of ministry, in young persons certainly, but also in all who show giftedness. What if the elders were to encourage each gift, to provide opportunities for service, and to guide gifted persons in the effective development and use of their gifts? If that were happening regularly, there would probably be little need for the July 1979 conference to discuss the crisis in Quaker leadership.

Suppose the elders really released Friends for ministry wherever that might take them. In too many situations "public Friends" have become so burdened by pastoral care and administration that effective gifts in preaching and teaching languish. Far too often "released Friends" have become captive Friends bound to the service of those who theoretically are releasing them. Some Friends meetings, on the other hand, have actively encouraged their pastors to take time to write for the larger public or to travel in the ministry as they have opportunity and have lightened their load accordingly. This has benefited us all. What if the elders would work to find a creative new balance in these matters? What if the elders were in fact to release pastors to spend a significant amount of time ministering to needs outside of the immediate circle of the Friends meeting, and were to take greater responsibility for the internal care of the meeting?

Suppose the elders were more active in "watching over one another for good." Where they have been doing this through counseling, assisting families in crisis, visiting the sick and needy, and much more, new life has emerged.

Suppose we don't have to suppose. The best of our tradition, both historic and contemporary, shows that the elders are often the movers and shakers. Or is that Quakers? Indeed it is! Let's help them.

Elders and Schizophrenia

The word "elder" leads a double-life. As a noun, "elder" commands respect, for an elder is one who has gained the confidence and respect of other Friends. However, as a verb "elder" becomes a villain. Even the thought of "being eldered" prompts feelings akin to dread. Friends have now come to the place of graciously accepting becoming an elder but of shrinking from being eldered. This schizophrenic life of "elder," I fear, robs us of a vital part of our common life, for elders and eldering have often been cautiously consigned to very limited roles in modern Friends meetings.

We can readily understand why elders frightened or frustrated Quakers in the past. Some descriptions of the elders of old at work still intimidate us. Rufus Jones recounts the story of a group of elders who sat so still on the facing bench that they prompted a young boy to ask whether they were even alive. Yet, despite their statue-like appearance, they also displayed an almost uncanny knowledge about all that happened in the meeting for worship and in the larger life of the meeting. The elders knew all and they controlled all. This, at least, is the image offered by popular memory.

The facts are, of course, that the ancient elders partly deserve this image even though they often served very well. Sometimes they misunderstood discipline to mean punishment and hastily read Friends out of meeting. Sometimes the elders magnified insignificant legalisms only to lose sight of the more important matters of discipleship. Some elders delighted too much in watching over the lives of others and in exercising the authority with which they were entrusted. Though not universal (or perhaps even typical), there were serious abuses.

Contemporary caution about elders, however, does not respond simply to past abuses. Even if the popular traditions and jokes about eldering were less ominous, many contemporary Friends would balk at assigning a serious role to elders. The "do-your-own-thing" privatism of modern culture has affected all of us deeply. Many Friends have come to believe that they demonstrate both personal privilege and wisdom when they run their own lives absolutely independently of other persons. Too often this privatism has undercut our commitment to Christian community so thoroughly that we hesitate both to give and to receive encouragement and guidance. Perhaps the failures of yesteryear's elders do not restrict the proper role of modern elders nearly as much as the fact that many Friends today are not willing to trust their lives in any significant way to those in their meetings.

In spite of our reluctance, it is essential to recover the best of what eldering means and to affirm it in our time. The practice of eldering was and potentially is one of the greatest strengths of a vital Friends meeting.

At their best, elders maintained two guiding concerns. The first was that the Friends meeting should have sound, nurturing ministry and meetings for worship. Sometimes to accomplish this they served as a check on ministry that hindered rather than helped the meeting. More often, the elders found ways to encourage effective ministry and ministers, whether established or just emerging.

The second concern is captured well in the advice, "Watch over one another for good." The motive in this was not to meddle in each other's lives. Instead it was to help Friends in their living to grow in spiritual maturity and to honor Christ and the Gospel. In this concern the elders (or in some periods "overseers") carried out essentially a pastoral role.

Both the concern for ministry and worship and the concern for faithful living require constant attention. In fact these concerns are far too important to entrust them to only one or two persons (such as a pastor), no matter how capable they may be. On such vital matters leadership must be broadly shared. It is as important now as it has ever been that the role of the elders be effectively fulfilled. It is time now to disown the double-life of "elder" and to discover the vital ways in which elders can serve today.

Meeting **Together**

The Performance

Worship, some suggest, is a performance we give to God, a great acting out of praise, a dramatic declaration of truth whether in soliloquy or speaking chorus. In one way of thinking, at least, this should be the grandest show we can manage—lights, bright costumes, full orchestra, singers galore, and dancers careening dervishly in raptures of praise like a chorus line of Davids whirling before the Ark without care that he had long ago stripped away his Sunday best, the more freely to dance for God. God would smile and laugh, I think, to see his creatures delight in him even if, despite its outrageousness, this great show only begins to answer God's delight in us.

We rarely call in the choreographers, however, but settle instead for robed choirs rooted in their places, belting out grand anthems as well as they can. And for preachers urbanely intoning truth while peering over their wooden fortresses.

Sometimes, though, the show must go on. So we draw the curtain on the stage of our hearts, strike up the band, and bring on the dancers. Even the hidden recesses of our spirits are caught up by surprise into tears and laughter, gratitude and wonder until, mysteriously but tangibly, our little selves are in chorus with the birds and the trees, the seas and the galaxies, all in great cheering and fortissimos sung to God. And again God rejoices.

The experience of worship, however, is not always trumpets, tympani, and ecstatic dancers. At root it is being present to God in the hope that God will be present to us. It is to gamble that Jesus was telling the truth when he said, "Where two or three are gathered in my name, there am I in the midst of them." (Matthew 18:20 RSV)

It is a gamble, too, that if God does come, we won't be entirely consumed by divine power and anger, or even by overwhelming love.

So we come, vulnerable to the One whose hands hold the whole universe. We come with all that we are, stripped of any masquerade—with our little successes, with our silly pride, with our brokenness, our fears, our failures great and small. And here we wait—with the bodies we don't like, the secret shame we bear, the doubts that we have (even about being here). Here we wait to meet God, hoping that in the encounter love will prevail.

The wonder is—it always is—that love does prevail. God may light our most hidden reasons for guilt with a beacon, but as we turn to run, holy tenderness holds us there. "Even with this," we hear, "I've not given up on you." Or that searching presence may strip away our self-deception to reveal conniving selfishness in what we thought were noble motives. Yet as we blush, the word comes, "Even with this, I've not abandoned you."

Sometimes the encounter is as subtle as the brush of a light breeze. The solid dome which our doubts tell us seals us off from heaven may show only a hairline fracture, but in it is the promise of breaking. The gray-green thunderheads of life whose stillness strikes terror in our hearts may admit only the slightest shaft of light, but in that is the promise that light will conquer darkness. So hope is rewarded with just enough of a glimpse to nurture hope.

Sometimes waiting is rewarded with wonder, wonder washing over us like an unseen ocean breaker crashing over our backs, leaving foam in our hair. It is the wonder of love, the wonder of the tender power of God, the wonder of the grace of having life itself. It is the wonder of seeing that God has been in the midst of life all along—teaching, providing, letting us love and be loved.

So the gamble pays off. Expectancy is rewarded—with unconditional love, with conviction, with renewed hope, with wonder. Often, instead of shouts, God's presence melts us to tears, liquid joy tracing down our cheeks, and to silence. Yet in this quiet cacophony of joy, settled and serene, God also delights.

Perhaps, in the end, worship is not so much what we do, outwardly or inwardly, as what we allow God to do in us. Holy Expectancy. Vulnerability. The gamble that God will come in love. "Be still," comes the ancient song, "and know that I am God." (Psalm 46:10 KJ)

Prepare for Worship

Early Friends frequently testified to the power and winsomeness of their meetings for worship. Isaac Penington, for example, reported that Friends in worship were "like a heap of fresh and burning coals, warming one another, as a great strength, freshness and vigor of life flows into all."

Sometimes this is our experience as well, but not often enough. Though we may expect peaks and valleys in the life of worship (as there are in the life of private devotion), we still long for more richness than we experience. How can the life of worship be nurtured so that it more consistently fulfills our hopes?

The life of worship requires preparation. We cannot, of course, by force of technique compel Christ to meet us as if he were a genie required to appear whenever someone rubs the magic lamp. However, Christ is eager to make good the promise to be present with those who are gathered in his name. Preparing for worship means ordering our lives so that we come to the meeting for worship expectantly and receptively.

Both "programmed" and "unprogrammed" Friends tend to forget the importance of preparing for worship. "Programmed" Friends have too often adopted an audience mentality. Many rely too easily on the preparation of those designated to sing, pray, and preach as a guarantee of a meaningful worship experience. On the other hand, "unprogrammed" Friends too often have so feared preparation of any sort that it would seem irreligious to rely on anything but the inspiration of the moment in meeting.

Preparation for worship is everyone's responsibility. Only through constant cultivation can Friends maintain the receptivity and readiness that make consistently powerful meetings for worship possible. To defend one manner of worship against another misses the point. What matters most is not prepared sermons or the lack of them, but prepared persons.

Friends can prepare for meeting for worship daily through various spiritual disciplines. These include the life-giving, life-consuming discipline of constant worship and praise, what Brother Lawrence called "the practice of the presence of God." They include the life of private prayer, regular reading of the Bible and literature of devotion. The daily disciplines also include the learning of little obediences. Hearing and obeying Christ as he prompts us in the little matters of daily living prepare us to hear our Teacher in the meeting for worship.

We can also order our lives so that we will help rather than hinder the meeting. Sleepy or snoring Friends give and receive little in worship. Perhaps Saturday night schedules should be consciously designed to allow adequate rest before meeting. Arriving at meeting in a state of readiness may include not arriving breathlessly late (try early) or not just turning from distractions such as a family feud or the Sunday morning newspaper. Having entered the meeting room, Friends can assist themselves and others in worship by avoiding distracting discourtesies such as catching up on the week's small talk, constant paper shuffling, and so on. Friends throughout our history have rightly insisted on the central importance of the meeting for worship. It is the center of our common life, the time when we together encounter the source of our life and power—the Living Christ. Something so important commands our constant attention. Let's prepare for worship.

Stopwatch Silence

Perhaps sober Friends everywhere will forgive a little noise about silence. It is wholly reasonable, after all, to imagine that a Quaker kid who knew extraordinarily little about "silent worship" until after he had come of age might have some strong opinions about it. This one does, and is even brassy enough to think that the following list of pet peeves is not merely trivial. Abuses of our best insights rob us all. Without pause, then, we rush on to a list of favorite offenses.

Stopwatch silence. This is silence that either is so short that you need a stopwatch to capture it or is precisely timed so that it won't take too long on the program. Many congregations can finish their silent moments in two minutes flat or better, although I don't know of a certified time for the quickest Quakers. Others more generously schedule five (please, don't exceed seven) minutes of waiting before the Lord.

Quantity of time for "open worship" isn't the whole story (though I still haven't received my mail-order course on "Instant Centering Down"). But it is part of the story. People can hardly be gathered in expectant waiting for Christ's teaching if there isn't any waiting. When there is time for five to ten minutes of announcements and pulpit chit-chat, sermons ten minutes too long for their messages, and extraneous activities that have nothing to do with worship, but there is no time for "unprogrammed" waiting before God, actions speak volumes about our attitudes toward worship.

Somber moments of numbing Hammond organ music (and other orchestrated silences). Even though organs are new-fangled contraptions among Quakers (relatively speaking), they have a wonderful place in the ministry of music. However, even if it's not played in funeral home tremolo, organ music should not be used to limit or manipulate silent worship. After all, the Spirit's movement among the people may last longer than exactly one stanza of a slow hymn. Or Christ may want to prompt a person to think, pray, or speak in ways that are different from the tone or text of the hymn being played.

If we assume (as we used to, at least) that in these moments Christ teaches us freely and directly, then it is similarly inappropriate for one individual to guide the worshipers in what they should think and pray. The great conductor and prompter in thought and speech is Christ alone.

Promotions of potlucks and politics. Open worship is not a time for announcements of potlucks, weddings or Cub Scout meetings (though I've heard them all and more). Nor is it a time for mere political propagandizing. There are times in worship, no doubt, when people must speak directly to political issues and governmental policies, but these times are often cheapened by persons who are venting personal opinion, not speaking the word of the Lord. Those who speak must be clearly led by the Spirit rather than be merely relieving political indigestion in public.

Private retreats. Open worship is not a time for each individual to retreat into private meditation and prayer, hoping that no one will be rude enough to interrupt by speaking, although I have often seen this kind of privatism openly encouraged. It is only when the people of God are gathered together—in adoration, in expectant listening, in ready obedience—that the wonder of God's meeting with us can be fully realized. Only as our spirits join together under Christ's leadership can we know the blessedness of the "gathered meeting."

These abuses (and others which might be added) come most often from ignorance or forgetfulness of the best things Friends know, rather than from malice. Surely some people avoid the use of silent waiting because they are afraid it will make someone impatient or because they are unwilling to take the risks it requires. However, most nod, at least, toward discovering the "gathered meeting" in worship, even though they may not thoughtfully honor its conditions or principles in their regular meetings.

We would do well to recover in practice our conviction that Christ does come in the meeting for worship to teach his people himself. Although a period of silent waiting is not the only means through which Christ meets us, we are the poorer to ignore or trivialize it. With a spirit of liberty and expectancy we can continue to discover afresh the power of waiting quietly together before the Lord. It is a discovery always to be longed for.

Let's pocket our stopwatches.

Is Preaching Okay?

Right away most Friends will recognize that "Is Preaching Okay?" is not the right question. We have already learned from the mistakes of our past that we must not demean or reject vocal ministry. The important question is instead, "What kind of preaching is okay?"

We can easily miss this central question by asking secondary or artificial questions such as who should speak, when the message came to the speaker, whether it was prepared or impromptu, or whether it was artful or not. By asking the central question, "What kind of preaching is okay?" we address all Friends and recall our deepest concerns.

The kind of vocal ministry we can accept tells the truth, responds to Divine direction, and rises as a living witness from the heart.

We must care most of all that any vocal ministry tells the truth. Though we may desire messages that are clear, interesting, or well-crafted, the first question to ask is whether a message is true. Friends have sometimes fallen prey to the idea that messages brought in meeting become sacrosanct. This concession to uncritical individualism endangers the truth. Surely all speak the truth as nearly as they can, but no person, professional or otherwise, attains infallibility simply for daring to speak in meeting. Instead, messages must be received in love, tested, and (at times) purified so that all together may grow in maturity and in the knowledge of God. Because they know the traps of pride, cleverness, unwitting prejudice, and more, experienced ministers are among the first to cherish the community's testing and guidance. The meeting should constantly renew the old question, "Does truth prosper?"

Further, acceptable preaching responds to divine direction. A message may be true and, at the same time, wrong for a certain people or time. Those who speak must be particularly discerning and obedient at this point. They must ask questions like, "Is this message for this time and this people? Am I the one who must deliver it? Have I spoken what is necessary—no more, no less?" This sort of question checks those who speak because they fidget in the silence and those who speak merely out of duty. It also cautions those who speak out of personal pique or use meeting for worship as a forum to lobby for pet concerns. For any preaching to be okay, Christ must direct it. We would not repeat the damaging error of our Quaker forebears by insisting that persons can be led only immediately before they speak, but we must insist that all speaking should arise clearly at the prompting and under the leading of our Inward Teacher.

Finally, preaching that is okay, at its root, rises as a living witness from the heart. Friends have rightly rejected preaching that is mere craft. To manipulate words and texts and to squeeze them into gleaming generalizations and alluring alliterations must not stand substitute for preaching from a fresh inward knowledge of God. Those who merely cant the outlines, words, and insights of others must be challenged still by the question, "But what can *you* say?"

To insist on living ministry does not plead for slothful or careless preaching. Intentional mediocrity demonstrates only a poverty of spirit. Vocal ministry should be neither slapdash nor secondhand. It must instead be disciplined and distilled from a heart alive to God.

Henri Nouwen understood this when he wrote:

> "The question is not, 'Do I have time to prepare?' but, 'Do I live in a state of preparedness?' When God is my only concern, when God is the center of my interest, when all my prayers, my reading, my studying, my speaking, and writing serve only to know God better and to make him known better . . . then I can live in such a state of preparedness and trust that speaking from the heart is also speaking to the heart." (*The Genesee Diary*, p. 59)

Friends need now, as in the past, a strong vocal ministry. May we nurture together preaching that has its root in truth, in divine direction, and in the heart.

The Nonsense of the Meeting

Methodists and Baptists find Quaker business procedure quaint and intriguing, if impractical. Their skepticism enhances my (self-righteous?) delight in describing to them the "sense of the meeting" and seeking the mind of Christ together as a way of doing church business. How much better to follow God's leading together than to depend on the raw power of majority rule! It is so creative, practical, and unifying. To soften the appearance of blind idealism I do add that this Friends practice is not perfect. Like any other method this can be abused.

The conscience nags just a bit if I fail to confess that too often the sense of the meeting is overcome by the nonsense of the meeting. The nonsense of the meeting wears many disguises, but behind any mask it will frustrate God's purposes. If Friends are to progress faithfully, they must expose nonsense for what it is and reject it.

One type of nonsense is religious dirty politics. At a recent Quaker gathering, for example, a novice accidentally overheard (at length) several "weighty Friends" planning a series of speeches which they intended to give during a pending business meeting. They went over in detail the content, sequence, and timing of these speeches so that during the meeting each Friend would appear to be speaking spontaneously under the Spirit's leading. In meeting they played out their charade.

Equally frustrating and damaging are persons who appear to agree with the decision of the monthly meeting but set out to undermine it almost immediately at the meeting's adjournment. Some of these folk should rejoice that the phone company charges a flat fee and not by the number of calls. Experienced clerks could tell many stories of how Friends through dirty politics have tried to force their will on others instead of seeking with others the will of God.

The nonsense of the meeting is not always politics. Sometimes it is apathy. To neglect coming to know and to do God's will hinders us just as decisively, though more subtly, as actively ignoring it.

Friends everywhere commonly complain that too few persons attend meetings for business. They are right, of course. In many meetings a relatively small percentage of the members makes most of the decisions. The majority's neglect of meeting for business robs the whole meeting of insight and energy it could have were they to participate.

Another evidence of the nonsense of apathy is when Friends don't care enough to wrestle with hard issues decisively and patiently. Some Friends, for example, choose to vote when the meeting is not clearly in agreement rather than to work hard to arrive at a unified sense of the meeting. If they truly want to discern together God's leading, Friends know that times of sharp disagreement are the worst time to vote. True guidance requires working, waiting, and listening, not expediency or apathy.

Through politics, apathy, overdependence on human wisdom, and many other ways we can fail to know together God's will. The nonsense of the meeting can too easily supplant a community sense of genuine guidance.

Please don't show this column to any Methodists or Baptists. They might fail to understand that, when we are faithful to God and to one another, the Quaker way of doing meeting business is practical and powerful. Perhaps if we put aside the nonsense, the ideals would become reality. Then other Christians could see for themselves. And my conscience wouldn't nag.

More Nonsense

After the publication of the column "The Nonsense of the Meeting" several months ago, reader response increased markedly. (Two letters flooded my desk.) Of the numerous comments I received, most could be translated roughly, "By George (an unseemly Quaker oath!), you have something there, but you've forgotten some common nonsense."

One common bit of nonsense we overlooked is the practice of spending seemingly endless time on inconsequential matters, sometimes while ignoring important issues. For example, one reader reported that almost an entire business meeting was devoted to deciding where a mirror should be placed in the meetinghouse cloakroom. Others remember disputes over the color of the carpet or of the paint to be used in the meetinghouse.

Debates over a mirror and similar follies illustrate not only a warped perspective but also a lack of trust. The whole monthly meeting does not need to make every decision. On many matters the meeting should decide instead to trust appropriate individuals or groups to carry on its work. This often happens, of course, but Friends have been justly criticized for choking meetings for business with matters best delegated to others in trust.

Other readers raised the perennial criticism that Friends conduct their business too slowly. They are often right, though they would not be if Friends disciplined themselves more carefully in their business. Frankly, we may be too slow at times because we rush. Some hurry so quickly to speak that they fail to listen carefully to others. This leads to unnecessary repetition and quarrelsomeness. And it takes too much time. It is often more efficient to stop to listen than to rush to speak. We can be deliberate without being slow. Unfortunately, we often let nonsense bog us down.

The nonsense readers seem to dislike most is the obstructing of the meeting by those (another Quaker oath) who talk endlessly in order to get their own way. Such nonsensical behavior takes improper advantage of the meeting's proper concern not to run roughshod over minorities. It also betrays the common misunderstanding that unity in the meeting means unanimity. It does not. Sometimes the meeting must recognize selfish obstructionist behavior for what it is and move ahead.

In describing Friends practice at this point, Rufus Jones writes: "A speaker who obviously speaks without depth or insight, or who is minded to be stubborn and have his own selfish way, will usually carry little weight and will be discounted when 'the sense of the meeting' is gathered up." (*The Faith and Practice of the Quakers*, p. 67)

In spite of persistent abuses, Friends often conduct their business in a wonderfully heartening manner. Last summer during a visit to Western Yearly Meeting I observed Friends (with their remarkable clerk, Dan Carter) work through some very difficult issues with patience and loving sensitivity. It made me glad again that Friends have chosen to conduct their business as they have.

Edward Burrough's counsel from 1662 still may guide us. He advised Friends that all things should "be carried on in the wisdom, love and fellowship of God in gravity, patience, meekness, unity and concord . . . by hearing and determining every matter coming before you in love, coolness, gentleness, and dear unity . . ." (quoted in Helen Hole, *Things Civil and Useful*, p.100)

Let's shun nonsense.

The Threshing Meeting

One of the first peculiarly Midwestern festivals our family attended in Kansas was an antique steam thresher and tractor show. Accompanied by owners clad in striped denim overalls and caps, these lesser cousins of the old steam locomotive convene to puff and hiss, to spew ash, and to whistle shrilly, gloating, perhaps, that they have survived to recall the good old days.

Though they now harvest nostalgia and curiosity, these brawny threshers were surely welcomed with gladness as they relieved the arduous labor of separating wheat from chaff. Even now they stand as a reminder that for most of human history (and in many places still) the work of harvest has been hard hand labor.

The realities of the harvest call to mind the colorful language describing the work of the early Publishers of Truth. Friends Edward Burrough and Francis Howgill, for example, were said to have been "in the general meeting place among the rude world, threshing and ploughing." (Brayshaw, *The Quakers,* p.109) The harvesting image was common enough among early Friends that many of the meetings that were held publicly to preach the Gospel were called "threshing meetings." Though I know of no place this name is still used, it can still teach and challenge us.

One of the essential features of the threshing meeting is that in it Friends set out to harvest new converts, not to nurture the faithful. Appointed meetings for worship were held in smaller groups at other places and times. The threshing meting was for the curious, the seekers, and the hostile, and great crowds were sometimes gathered. Several thousand people might travel to meetings in the orchards or open fields, and not infrequently up to a thousand jammed into the great Bull and Mouth hall to hear, heckle, or argue with the upcountry Quaker preachers.

"Threshing the heathenish nature" in these settings was strenuous work, and only the strongest and most mature ministers were entrusted with it. To many it did not even seem appropriately religious. Some opponents of Friends scoffed at their meetings at the Bull and Mouth, calling the rented hall the "new hired great tavern chapel." Yet the meetings went on there and elsewhere with great effectiveness.

Even though the particular format of these gatherings may have been peculiarly appropriate to its time (just as the "revival meeting" was to mid-nineteenth century America), the timeless concern to gather people to obedience to Christ still prompts the question, "Where is the threshing meeting today?" We should hardly be pleased when others, seeing our timidity in declaring the Truth, compliment us on our exceedingly fine religious manners. Nor should we be satisfied to proclaim the Gospel only in our meetinghouses or churches and only to the faithful. That's not threshing. It's only stirring stored grain.

Under the Spirit's guidance, Friends must discover ways appropriate to our time to plough new ground and to separate the wheat from the chaff in order to gather a harvest. Strong, mature Friends need to be charged with this work. Bold, probably unconventional, approaches will be required to send us into the fields that are, in fact, ready for harvest. Whatever that means, those who have never heard of the Living Christ present in power have a right to hear. Those whose life is Christ must be eager to tell them.

Let's re-invent the threshing meeting for our time.

The Meeting for Clearness

One was facing a watershed decision in his career. Another sought guidance about her ministry and how to prepare most effectively for its new direction. A young couple wanted to seek the counsel of others about whether they should be married. In each instance, these persons called together a group of Friends in a "meeting for clearness" in order to discern God's guidance. Such stories could be multiplied across the family of Friends, as could the accounts of how helpful these small gatherings are. The meeting for clearness is an impressive, though simple, way of discovering God's leading. Indeed, it is such an effective and loving means that it is surprising that we do not use it more frequently. Surely it deserves to be restored to a more prominent place in our life together.

Most simply, the meeting for clearness arises when a person needing guidance asks spiritually discerning Friends to join in his or her search for God's leading. The gathering is conducted in a spirit of worship with ample time provided in order to prevent a sense of hurry. Prayer penetrates the whole process, not only beginning and concluding the meeting, but often being turned to in the midst of discussion. In this context, the important issues are presented, questions asked, options explored, motives tested and more. What has impressed me most is that the result of this deliberation is generally wiser and more creative than any ideas with which the group began. As God empowers it, this process works wonderfully.

The meeting for clearness gets results and that surely should be reason enough to use it. But it also reminds us of how much we need others in the community of faith. It expresses concretely the fact that we cannot live for Christ in isolation but need instead the direction, correction and encouragement of our Christian brothers and sisters.

On the one hand, it is important that we recognize our own weakness. Each of us needs to admit that we don't always receive the Light unfiltered and that we may have points of blindness. Everett Cattell helpfully reminds us that even Amos Kenworthy, legendary for his spiritual insight, submitted himself to others to guide his ministry. None of us is beyond that need.

On the other hand, we also need to recognize the strength that we have together. Friends have long affirmed that we are wiser together than alone as we listen for God's direction. The meeting for clearness is a specific expression of the strength of our common life.

In *Prayer is a Hunger*, Edward Farrell speaks helpfully to our need for one another:

> "Most of us are fairly knowledgeable in helping people or doing things for people. Too often what we fail to do is allow others to reach us, to teach us, to be gifts to us, to experience our need for them. We learn this truth with great pain because we spend much of our lives trying to become independent. When we reach this point, we find out how inadequate autonomy is. Then we have to start all over again, allowing people to know how incomplete we are without them." (pp. 75–76)

To live without the counsel of others may be considered by some to be a healthy independence, but it is more likely an expression of pride, of an autonomy that destroys rather than builds.

In recent months it has been particularly delightful to watch the joy of discovery that new Friends have found in the meeting for clearness. Because it is effective and because it points to our need for one another, I hope many more will learn its power.

The Meeting for Learning

Until recently I thought I had heard about every sort of Friends "meeting" there could be. This delusion quickly disappeared when some fellow conferees talked with enthusiasm about the "meeting for learning." Friends probably don't need to proliferate specialized language, but this term, credited to Parker Palmer of Pendle Hill, deserves our attention. "Meeting for learning" immediately evokes for me the importance of learning as a part of Christian experience, the importance of the learning fellowship, and the inseparability of learning from constant attention to Christ our Teacher.

Two opposite dangers undermine a clear appreciation of the importance of learning in the meeting. On the one hand, learning has sometimes become sterile intellectualizing which hinders or replaces faith. On the other hand, there is a false spirituality (which occurs among all sorts of Friends—fundamentalists to humanistic mystics) that asserts that to know facts or to use reason is beneath the true saint. Both hazards threaten the truth. A dynamic, enduring faith is one that grows though both intellectual and spiritual experience.

Learning about our faith helps to deliver us from "goosebump religion" in which we rely almost wholly on our feelings. It helps to deliver the Christian from misleading errors which could cut the nerve of faithful living. Beyond its preventative value, however, learning can lead into new depths of spiritual experience. It is no accident that many of Christendom's spiritual giants have also been intellectual giants—Paul, Augustine, Luther and Pascal, for example, and leading Friends in all periods of our own history.

The term "meeting for learning" suggests the importance not only of learning itself but also of the learning fellowship. Just as many fruit trees require cross-pollinization if they are to bear fruit (and almost all benefit from it), so Christian learners become healthier and more productive when they learn together.

We have often thought that "fellowship" happens only before or after learning experiences, while we are sipping coffee and swapping jokes and gossip. But this is quite mistaken. On the contrary, we can come to have a special delight in and appreciation for one another as we share ideas and insights or as we struggle through (or even argue through) life's big questions together. Some of the friends I cherish most are those who will, out of the freshness of their own learning, share new insights and ask penetrating questions about God and the life of obedience. I need them. We all need each other.

Even standing together, we must ultimately depend on Christ to teach us. "Meeting for learning" reminds us that we still must approach living and learning in humble obedience. Without this our best efforts will fail. But there is great hope, for Christ still comes "to teach his people himself."

The term "meeting for learning" may pass (I hope not), but its significance must endure. A people that knows God with both heart and mind can, with God's help, powerfully advance God's good purposes in our world.

Nurturing **Ministry**

Fit for Ministry

The Quaker concept of ministry, historically one of Friends most useful contributions to the larger Christian community, has fallen on hard times. Between the poles of those who recognize no ministers and those who adopt a Protestant pastoral system, Friends have great confusion about who a minister is, how a minister functions, and how individuals become prepared for ministry. The last question has become one of increasing importance.

The question of preparation for ministry has opposite dangers, both of which must be rejected in favor of an important principle that Friends have understood from the beginning.

Education does not fit one for ministry. The modern craze for credentialing and certification in all areas of life might mislead us to think that education can produce ministers. Yet it is perfectly clear that it cannot. One of George Fox's earliest insights was that "ministers are not made at Oxford and Cambridge," the elite theological schools of that time.

Experience tells us that many powerful ministers of Christ have not had the benefit of formal education. The Apostle Peter spoke powerfully at Pentecost without having taken a course in homiletics. As far as we know, the first great missionary, Paul, had no training in cross-cultural evangelism or pastoral methods, although he was a learned man. The Quakers Valiant Sixty could not have qualified for a seminary degree between them.

Experience also teaches us that theological education is no guarantee of effective ministry. After all, many Friends meetings have endured the lifeless efforts of theologically-educated bumblers who differ from their uneducated counterparts principally in knowing bigger words with which to excuse their mistakes.

Similarly, ignorance does not fit one for ministry. Some of our most serviceable ministers have been very well-educated, from the important leaders of earlier centuries such as William Penn, Robert

Barclay, Joseph John Gurney to widely-read Quaker author-ministers of this century—Rufus Jones, Douglas Steere, Thomas Kelly, Elton Trueblood and Richard Foster. They have been able to minister out of their learning.

We have seen too often a kind of presumption in ignorance, usually very sincere, which masquerades as dependence on the Spirit. This, too, fails us. Lack of learning is no demonstration of piety.

There is a tangible content to the Christian faith in which ministers (and all others) need to be grounded. These include, at least, a grasp of the biblical roots of faith, a theological framework in which to understand and to communicate the experience of faith and experiential knowledge of the paths of devotion, prayer and worship. Knowledge of content and disciplined thinking can help ministers transcend theological sentimentalism of any style.

At our best, Friends have insisted that Christ fits one for ministry. In ways that are tailored to each individual's call, Christ prepares and empowers each one for service.

The root of such preparation is the knowledge of God. "The principal and required qualifications," writes Robert Barclay, "are the power, life, and virtue of the Spirit, and the pure grace which comes from it." The commitment to hear and obey Christ is essential to any life-giving ministry. Without it, education is irrelevant. Without a passion for God, ministers become mere hirelings and false guides.

The life of obedience becomes the basis of preparation. I am completely persuaded that those who will hear and obey Christ will be adequately prepared for any service for which they are chosen. We should not expect (or require) that all preparation be the same, for not all ministers are called to serve in the same way. How much better it would be if committees on ministry would help each individual discern not only the particular service but also the specific preparation to which he or she is called.

In the end, we must steer a course between relying on education and cherishing ignorance. Neither option serves us well. Instead, we must learn that Christ in love and wisdom will equip each individual perfectly for ministry in the power of God.

What Do You Know by Heart?

In sharp criticism of theological education in his day, Robert Barclay wrote:

> "One who is going to be a minister must learn this art
> or trade of merchandising with the scriptures. . . . All
> of this [theological training] is done so that the trained
> minister can acquire a knack of taking a verse of scripture
> and adding his own barren notions and conceptions
> to it. He also adds what he has stolen from books, and
> for this purpose he has to have a great many. Then on
> each Sabbath-day, as they call it, or oftener, he makes an
> hour-long discourse. This is called 'preaching the word.'"
> (*Barclay's Apology in Modern English*, pp. 204–205)

This quotation, taken from one of the great many books in my own library, could make one feel defensive or guilty for having and prizing a theological education. What it should do instead is help us to see more clearly the relationship between education and ministry. Many Friends today are struggling with this issue to understand how our tradition meets modern times. Perhaps some of the following principles can help.

First, Christ prepares people for ministry (whether pastoral or other forms). This is simple, but it is also the single most important principle to remember. Friends from the beginning have insisted that Christ not only calls and ordains people to ministry but that he also prepares and empowers them for their ministry. This does not claim that people can minister effectively without preparation. Instead, it recognizes the genuinely necessary preparation. In the words of Joseph John Gurney:

> "The work of grace, which is carried forward in the hearts
> of his selected servants, by the Lord himself, is deemed
> by Friends to be at once indispensable and sufficient, as a
> preparation for the Christian ministry." (*A Peculiar People*,
> p. 220)

Christ's preparing work may take many forms. Christ teaches us in personal experiences, in the life of devotion, in the study of the Bible, in our worship together, and in many other ways. All of these avenues may lead to the kind of knowledge, understanding, and spiritual maturity that make effective ministry possible. We must remain open to all the means of Christ's work. Indeed, in contrast to Barclay, we may even suggest that faithfulness to Christ's call and preparatory work will lead some (or even many) to formal theological education. On the other hand, we must not insist that this will be true for all.

Another basic insight is that spiritual giftedness and formal education may have no relationship to one another. The Bible gives us no indication that gifts in the ministry are reserved for the educated. The biblical record, in fact, is filled with stories of how God powerfully used the least likely to succeed and the least well prepared (according to common standards). For example, the rough Galilean apostles stood in sharp contrast with the superbly educated clergy of their time. In our own history, the Valiant Sixty of the Quaker explosion were mostly humble folk whom God used mightily much to the chagrin of the acceptable Cambridge and Oxford trained clergy. To insist that today God can minister only through educated persons is a heresy denied by both the Bible and the history of the Church. On the other hand, to say that God cannot use educated persons would be equally false.

As a college and seminary teacher, I do not intend to undercut formal training. I value it greatly, but I also know some of its potential traps. Instead, I hope to point us back to the essentials. We must not limit God's work through a falsely narrow view of ministry. In evaluating our ministry, we must not substitute formal credentials or artificial standards for spiritual discernment. Ultimately we must ask our ministers what we ought to ask ourselves: "What do you know by heart?

A Case (Cassette?) for Recording

Most Friends recognize that a "cassette ministry" is not what we mean by "recording" persons in the ministry. Unfortunately, many Friends (among both those who "record" and those who do not) cannot as easily describe what "recording in the ministry" is. This is a great loss since "recording" is woven into the fabric of our understanding of ministry. Frayed ideas at this point will surely injure the whole cloth.

Basically, "recording" is the formal recognition by a meeting of a gift in public ministry demonstrated in action over a sustained period of time. Though a bit awkward, like many definitions, this statement includes what is essential.

The practice of formally recognizing certain gifts grew out of need and is still useful. Recognition potentially increases effectiveness. In the local meeting such recognition encourages persons to use their gifts. In effect we say, "God has given you public gifts which we need. We urge you to use them freely under God's guidance." In broader circles, such recognition is a way of commending these persons' ministry to Friends and others who don't know them. Recording these gifts in ministry is a practical way to broaden their usefulness.

Traditionally Friends have recorded gifts in public ministry such as preaching, teaching, and (more recently) skill in pastoral care. Because these gifts are so visible, recognition both encourages the gifted and protects Friends in some measure from self-proclaimed leaders whose service is not from a spiritual root or consistent with Friends insights. From the beginning Quakers have been concerned that the Friends movement not be discredited by a few individuals who are "out of the Truth."

Dangers exist, of course, in recognizing these public gifts. Some may think that gifts of preaching or teaching are more worthy than other spiritual gifts. Others may suppose that "recorded" persons with these public gifts do or should have more status than others. Unfortunately, Friends have sometimes made both of these mistakes. At our best, however, we know that Paul was right when he eloquently argues in I Corinthians 12 that gifts are different only in function, not in status. Recording should not give special status or pride of place. That is why it is so important when we talk about recording to avoid priestly language such as "set apart," "specially chosen by God" or "high-calling," all of which wrongly suggest that the gifts of public ministry confer special honor, status, or divine favor. Public gifts need to be recognized, but not because they are better than other gifts.

Another long-standing principle in recording public gifts is that Friends simply recognized the effective exercise of those gifts. Recording does not certify that one is ready to begin ministry. Instead it points out ministry in action. When a person's effective service has demonstrated that God has ordained him or her to the ministry, then Friends can record that giftedness. In this way, Friends differ from many other Christians who tend to inaugurate a person's ministry with ordination.

Several modern errors are weakening the practice of recording. On the matter of recording and status, some Friends have in fact elevated the status of recorded ministers while others have given up recording altogether, trying (in part) to avoid giving status. Both groups have diminished the effectiveness and breadth of their ministry.

Another error is the increasing tendency in some yearly meetings for recording committees to act as training committees. There surely is a proper place for the nurture of emerging gifts, but this task must not be confused with the task of recognizing demonstrated gifts in ministry. The educational prerequisites to recording in several yearly meetings fall prey to this confusion.

Finally, in recent decades there has been a misleading professionalization of recording. It is almost as if some (at least) think that if one gets paid for ministry, one is gifted; if one is not paid, then he or she is not gifted. This is a foolish and debilitating error.

Many Friends today are considering anew the meaning and usefulness of recording ministers. It is right that they are. A sound understanding of recording is important to an effective Friends ministry. Let's record thoughtfully and with discernment.

Nothing Against Women, But . . .

For advocates of unrestricted opportunity for women in the church, the over 300-year heritage of Friends has been commonly cited as an example of the effective use of women's spiritual gifts. It is a proud heritage. Well-known women such as Elizabeth Hooton, Mary Dyer, Margaret Fell, Elizabeth Fry, Hannah Chapman Backhouse, and Sybil Jones represent only a fraction of the Friends women who have contribute greatly to Christ's work in the world.

Many Friends today are convinced that, in spite of this heritage, opportunities for women to minister among Friends have declined significantly in recent decades. Several observations suggest that this conclusion is justified.

Research done in 1979 by Paula Teague reveals a great disparity between opportunities for men and women among Friends. For example, in the largest American yearly meeting only one percent of all pastors *and* clerks are women. Other Friends United Meeting yearly meetings (among pastoral Friends) follow closely with one at three percent, two at five percent, and the highest at fifteen present. (New England and New York Yearly Meetings, which rely more heavily on clerks, show a higher percentage of women as pastors and clerks.)

Among the FUM yearly meetings that record ministers, the percentage of all recorded persons who are women is similarly low. The highest percentage among the yearly meetings was seventeen percent with several between seven and ten percent. The superintendent of one of these yearly meetings cannot recall a woman being recorded in his yearly meeting for more than twenty-five years! If this represents an extreme, it also represents a trend. In some yearly meetings there are very few recorded women under sixty years of age, which indicates that in recent decades we have been quite reluctant to record women. Paula Teague's research also bears out this analysis.

More anecdotally, even today there are Friends leaders who advise young women who feel a call to ministry to marry a minister rather than to try to live out that call directly. The sad record of the past is that where such advice has been followed, it has often, though not always, been very damaging both to the individuals involved and to the community of Friends. This is disturbing, but not unexpected. We should not be surprised when not following the divine call (even at the encouragement of others) produces shame, guilt, bitterness, and even rage with their far-reaching consequences.

This is not simply a faddish concern for quotas or statistics. It is a concern for individuals and for the church. Friends have insisted, both because of the teaching and example of the biblical tradition and because of their own rich experience, that women as well as men are entrusted with special gifts of ministry and that these gifts should be encouraged, recognized, and used.

Why, then, have opportunities for women declined? The reasons are many and complex. One reason may be an un-Christian and unmerited capitulation to cultural expectations, as in the statement, "I have nothing against women in ministry, but, let's be practical, they wouldn't be accepted in our culture." Another reason may be that in adopting the pastoral system, many also adopted mistakenly the notion that pastors must be male. More recently, some Friends have adhered increasingly to an authoritative biblicism which, at least on this issue, has distorted the biblical message itself. These and other reasons have contributed to limiting the ministry of women.

It is especially ironic that Friends have offered women gradually fewer opportunities while other Christians are beginning to increase opportunity. In a time when more and more women are taking the risk of developing their spiritual gifts, Friends must seriously consider their practice at this point. To deny anyone the full expression of her God-given gifts is no trivial offense. It blocks the will of God for gifted individuals and for us all.

The Abraham Farrington Society

Friends need to establish some Abraham Farrington Societies, says Ben Richmond (according to Dan Treadway). Farrington, Ben observes, embodied an important model of encouraging the ministry when he, an established minister, took young John Woolman with him to "hold forth the Word of Life" in the mostly Presbyterian region surrounding Brunswick, New Jersey. Good point.

Personally, I would hesitate to found such a group without prior permission from its namesake. However, were that obtained, there are at least two ideas that I would urge Farringtonians to remember as they try to encourage the ministry.

Open your eyes. Be alert to those whom God is moving toward ministry in order to recognize and affirm their emerging giftedness. Attentiveness here must include expecting the unexpected, perhaps with one eye turned toward the improbable. We see in hindsight that Jesus' disciples (and later the Valiant Sixty) were among the least likely to "turn the world upside down," but we tend to forget this as we think about people whom God would use today. There is tremendous mischief in holding destructively narrow expectations about who God's ministers should be. For example, it is less a slip of the tongue than betrayal of the heart when committees on ministry talk with anticipation only about the "young men" who are to come under their care. I know of no reason biblically or historically that we should expect all or most new ministry to occur among men or among younger people. Yet here, as elsewhere, we see too narrowly because of the blinders of limited expectation.

Open your heart. A steady devotion to God is prerequisite to being able to see and liberate the ministry of others. The work of God within us allows us to see the work of God around us. Spiritual giftedness is most aptly recognized by those who know God.

It is also in the context of the life of devotion that God can reveal to us and shatter our inner barriers that resist the ministry of others. Some may want to discourage God's work in others in order to sidestep God's call on themselves. Some recognized ministers may be tempted (perhaps unwittingly) to save their encouragement for those who, like themselves, have "paid their dues" educationally or in other ways. More simply (and subtly), some may be hindered by pride that prevents them from seeing and rejoicing in God's gifts to others. Such attitudes seem odd for those who follow Jesus, who rejected pride of place and rejoiced that his disciples' works would surpass his own. Christ's inward teaching would open our hearts still to delight in the spiritual giftedness of others.

Recognizing and receiving the ministry of others is only a first step, one to be followed by practical steps of nurture and encouragement. But it is an important first step, for without this our other efforts to encourage the ministry will widely miss the mark. Abraham Farrington set a good example for Woolman and for us, and we would do well to follow his lead.

Praying for Leaders

The early morning phone calls telling of a tragic airplane crash near Greensburg, Kansas, stunned us, of course, and we still feel keenly the loss of David Leach, Sheldon Louthan and Delmar Day, wonderful friends and valued leaders. Our bewilderment has been even greater as we have remembered how many leaders we have lost through death or impairment in the last few years. Friends everywhere feel deeply our common loss.

One response to this loss has come urgently enough and often enough that it ought to be shared broadly. Independently, Friends from several parts of the country have repeated the concern that we must pray for our leaders. We are in spiritual warfare (Ephesians 6) and we must bring spiritual resources to bear in order to protect and sustain our leaders. Even as "the power of the Lord" often guarded and opened the way for George Fox and his companions, so it can continue to prevail in our everyday lives. Our prayers can help release "the power of the Lord" for our leaders in several specific areas.

First of all, we can pray for our leaders' health and well-being. Ask that they be guarded from violence and accidents and that they be protected from diseases that would diminish their effectiveness. Certainly none of us is immune to the effects of evil in the world but prayer can limit its power. More positively, we can ask that leaders grow in their ability to order their lives under divine guidance so that they will make wise decisions for health and wholeness in all areas of their living.

Similarly, we can pray that our leaders will have whole, nurturing relationships. Those who have families, for example, need them to be loving environments filled with harmony and mutual encouragement. Marital stress or serious conflict with children burdens and limits leaders. So does fighting with members of the meetings and organizations that they serve. How much better to pray together, even in times of disagreement, than to let antagonism grow! The Friends tradition of seeking guidance together in a spirit of worship is a wise, relevant precedent.

Because many of our leaders suffer isolation and loneliness, we ought also to pray that they be given friendships which affirm them and help them to see life bigger than their duties. Good friends help build wholeness.

We can also pray that our leaders continually grow deeper in the inner life. Though it may be less visible, this is a place that spiritual battles rage. Attacks here can render one ineffective. Discouragement or a sense of worthlessness can rob one's energies. Early vision and enthusiasm can deteriorate into a business-as-usual complacency and a loss of nerve. Not uncommonly, leaders are weakened by pride or by such an eagerness to please everyone that they compromise Truth.

To prevent these and other wounds of the spirit, we should pray that our leaders will live steadily in joy, that they grow in both patience and dreams of the possible, and that they discern ever more clearly the spiritual realities around them. We can ask that they be drawn deeply into the Divine Center from which flows both the humility to submit to others and the boldness to act faithfully in the face of opposition. The inner life can be lifted through our prayers.

As I have traveled among Friends over the last several years, many have lamented an apparent low ebb of leadership among us. At the same time I have been moved by the fact that many Friends leaders are rarely or never supported in prayer by those who look to them to set the pace. These two observations are related. We are now paying the price of carelessness in prayer.

The Apostle Paul concluded his discussion of spiritual warfare with this instruction and request: "Pray all the time, asking for what you need, praying in the Spirit on every possible occasion. Never get tired of staying awake to pray for all the saints; and pray for me to be given an opportunity to open my mouth and speak without fear and give out the mystery of the gospel of which I am an ambassador in chains; pray that in proclaiming it I may speak as boldly as I ought to." (Ephesians 6:18–20, JB)

In this spirit let's pray for one another and especially for our leaders.

Practical **Distinctives**

Family Resemblance

"What difference does it make from whom anyone is descended?" William Penn asked impertinently. (*No Cross, No Crown*, Selleck ed., p. 71) Obviously a first-generation Quaker, Penn would blindly slight the importance of standing seven generations deep as a Starbuck, Coffin, Newlin, Hinshaw, Roberts or other gray-gilded family.

We must admit, of course, the seamier side of the heritage game. For example, some folk use genealogical blackmail. "If you don't do it my way, I'll prove we're related" can be a genuine threat. Lack of lineage poses problems, too. In some meetings, more recently convinced Friends can remain newcomers for several generations.

The larger Quaker family has also struggled with genealogy. One group will debate with another over whose lineage is purer, even to the point of libeling the dead.

Such quarreling has not been productive, of course, but does raise again the question, "Who, indeed, are the true Quakers?" Were Penn living today, he surely would care little for lines of descent, whether of family or faction. Neither would John the Baptist who warned some roots-conscious Jewish contemporaries, "Do not think of telling yourselves, 'We have Abraham for our father,' because, I tell you, God can raise children for Abraham from these stones." (Luke 3:8, JB) Many years ago Friends quit recognizing individuals as "birthright" members because they wanted to say clearly that secondhand religion is not good enough. Birthright religion is equally fraudulent for a people. True Quakers are not necessarily those whose ancestors knew God.

The inheritance and mantle of Friends rightly falls only to those who live in the same life and power in which the first Friends lived. It belongs to those who know Christ for themselves, to those who know by experience that Christ still acts powerfully in the world calling out a daring people, renewing what is lifeless and broken, and advancing the influence of the Kingdom of God. Authentic Quakers in any generation care more about firsthand religion than "old-time religion."

Anything less mocks the great spiritual legacy that Friends cherish.

Not long ago I read of a young woman who "had some hesitation about becoming a Quaker for fear that she could not live up to it." She felt, as many families do, that there is a certain standard or spirit which family members must meet. Not a few parents have sent teenagers off for an evening with "Now remember you're a Jones (Brown, Thornburg, etc.)."

In a way, our Quaker ancestors call after each generation, "Now remember, you're a Friend." For us that requires more than merely dusting the old family photographs or despising the voice as it calls. It asks instead for a living up to the best we have known. The finest treasures in the inheritance can be neither invested nor spent, for they are lives lived beautifully and wholly for God. We become Quaker sons and daughters by living with the same eager devotion.

To patriarch Penn we grant the last word: "God neither likes nor dislikes by heredity. Nor does he regard what people were, but what they are." (*No Cross, No Crown*, p. 83)

Checklists for Extraordinary Ordinary Living

"Queries" is an odd word now. It amuses us sometimes, but mostly "queries" seems like a word from another era. The danger is that if the word seems quaint, the practice of using these questions about the life of faithfulness might also seem out-dated. Partly to guard against the inadvertent loss of this useful practice, Mid-America Yearly Meeting several years ago changed the word "queries" to "checklist." Though neither elegant nor religious in tone, "checklist" sounds practical, precisely as it should. The use of questions about life and faith is very down-to-earth and should be made as useful as possible.

In reading the queries, one notices immediately how they focus attention on practical living. Many of the questions begin, "Do you

. . . ?" or, "What are you doing . . . ?" about various facets of our lives. They emphasize the life of acted faith. One must have not mere belief, but also a believable life. Belief is not unimportant, but it is insufficient. Followers of Christ must model his life in everyday living. The queries remind us of that by asking, "What are you doing?"

Even though the queries have an open-endedness for individuals, they also offer guidance and bring some obligation. Part of their practical value is that they gather up the collective wisdom and spiritual insight of groups of Friends, both historic and contemporary. They are a sort of community standard which should teach each individual even while they avoid legalistic moralism.

The queries also prove valuable because they encourage responsible self-examination. Most of us prefer to avoid that. The disciplined use of these challenging questions can block our evasions and draw us toward extraordinary ordinary living.

Several steps might be taken to make the queries even more useful. An obvious step is to make sure that the questions themselves are contemporary, crisp, direct, and unambiguous. Some phrasings of questions seem to me to be too "religious" and too easily ignored. The questions are practical. They should sound practical. Queries for children often capture this tone better than the rest. For example, "Do you try to be honest and truthful in what you say and do? Do you stand firmly against acts that are sneaky and underhanded? . . . Do you try to find out what God wants you to be and to do?" (*New England Yearly Meeting Faith and Practice*, 1966, p. 206) Simple specific questions guide us helpfully and expose pretense in the life of acted faith.

Another way of making the queries serviceable is to consider them just a few at a time instead of all at once. Too often they are read too quickly and at too much length to allow serious reflection under Christ's leadership.

Finally, to be as useful as possible, the queries should be readily accessible. Instead of leaving them buried in Faith and Practice books,

Friends could copy them out individually on cards to be left in various places where they would often be seen—near a desk, on a window sill, on a closet door. Meeting newsletters or bulletins could (and some do) include one or two in each of their issues. Perhaps some artistic and enterprising Friends could even design some attractive posters using queries.

The queries are still a very practical checklist for faithful living. Let's ponder them often and make them as useful as possible.

The Honest Truth

The redundant phrase "the honest truth" warns immediately that the truth may not always be told. Even though there aren't corresponding phrases such as "the dishonest truth" or "the almost honest truth," deceit often intrudes on our everyday lives. This fact shocks only the thoroughly naïve. What is alarming, however, are the indications that integrity may be in sharp decline in our time.

Evidences of this decline confront us frequently. In a recent television interview, a researcher reported on an experiment in which 75 of 100 persons failed to act honestly in as simple a situation as going through a grocery check-out stand. The researcher himself not only studies deception, but defends it. Sissela Bok's practical book, *Lying*, though not defending deceit, shows how widespread the problem is both for individuals and institutions. From "Almost Honest John's" used car lot in Portland, Oregon, to the halls of government in Washington, D.C., "the honest truth" often seems to have disappeared. Individuals in many walks of life know that the pressure to conform to almost routine deceit is very great. Really!

Precisely on this issue the traditional Quaker trait of integrity can encounter contemporary culture in a striking way. Ever since George Fox insisted that Jesus was serious when he said, "Let your yes be yes, and your no, no," honesty has been a Quaker hallmark. Jailers trusted Quaker prisoners to walk unguarded from one jail to another. Friends shopkeepers and artisans prospered when their neighbors learned how reliable they were. This distinctive reputation for integrity, well-deserved, lingers even today in numerous brand name products. (Have you ever heard of Presbyterian Oats? Or Baptist Motor Oil?) Truth requires that we humbly admit that Friends were not the only honest Christians. Yet it was of our forebears they used to say, "A Quaker's word is as good as his bond."

My father taught me that the old adage about a Quaker's word was not a mere relic of the past. I hope that I can teach my children and grandchildren the same thing. In an age of deceit, Friends can stand as a beacon to integrity. A life lived in straightforward truthfulness is, in the end, very winsome. It joins our sense of what ought to be with a demonstration of what can be. It shows that honest living is both practical and possible. Even more, such a life points beyond itself to the Truth which we have experienced and which is the foundation for all of our living. This witness is worth making.

Because dishonesty is so prevalent, we know that maintaining integrity, as important as that is, is not always easy. Blatant lies ("little white" or otherwise) can be readily refused, but there are subtler deceits. Some are tempted to exaggerate (stretch) the truth in ways that distort it, even in a good cause. Others, in deference to certain tastes in etiquette, take up fawning flattery as a means to their ends. The Quaker inclination to understatement ("How's your wife?" "She seems to be as she sometimes is.") may also obscure the truth. Sometimes in our Friends gatherings we adopt an ambiguous vocabulary of polite, mutually-agreed-upon deception. Temptation to adopt "the almost honest truth" lurks everywhere. Nonetheless, even with its difficulties, one can live a life of integrity in the power of Christ.

Quaker lives should make the phrase "the honest truth" unnecessary.

The Rev. Dr. George Fox

"I am highly privileged to introduce to you tonight," begins the speaker, "one of our most eminent ministers. He is a missionary, an evangelist, a pastor, and an author of numerous pamphlets and letters (which many of you have read). He is known throughout the British Isles, on the Continent, in America and the Caribbean. He has been consulted by heads of state and has often suffered valiantly for his convictions. We are all deeply in his debt for his profound faith. Welcome with me now our guest speaker, the Reverend Doctor George Fox."

If such a scene is jarring, it is not because we cannot imagine it happening among Friends today. We can also imagine George Fox scolding the speaker for such fawning flattery. After all, Dr. Fox and his associates had suffered imprisonment for refusing to join in the exaggerated manners of showing honor and respect in their time.

Going to jail for failing to tip one's hat may seem odd to us, and since the customs of hat honor, bowing and curtsying, and honorific titles such as "most excellent," "your grace," and "right worshipful" have passed, the traditional Friends concern about giving honor may well seem wholly irrelevant.

The question of how to show respect, however, is not merely a curiosity in a Quaker "Believe-it-or-Not" Museum. Though customs of honor have changed, the human spirit has not. The pride that craves honor remains, as does the self-serving eagerness to please others or to gain favors, which leads to flattery. The issue of showing honor is important because it is a practical testing ground for our pride and honesty.

Opposition to certain practices may make Friends out to be grumpy or rude, yet helpful caution grows out of even a negative approach to this problem. Simply stated, Christians should avoid using or expecting forms of respect which are false or exaggerated, which feed pride, or which are designed to gain favor.

For example, Friends have traditionally avoided the use of honorific titles such as "Reverend," "Doctor," or "The Honorable." Their use panders to pride, while being unnecessary and full of subtle dangers. Though I have tried, I can hardly imagine that to the man who had called him "good teacher" Jesus would respond, "Why do you call me good? I prefer to be called 'Reverend.'" In my experience, the struggle over whether to address others by title has more to do with protecting my ego than with showing respect to the other person.

Similarly, public and private introductions of others can be terribly misused. Far too often, I suspect, the puffed-up language of introductions is intended to curry favor with the one being introduced or to impress the listeners with one's own importance by virtue of having distinguished friends or acquaintances.

Flattery, though it need not be public, is another common abuse in showing honor. It is to use, in William Penn's words, "empty and fictitious" language to describe a person as greater than he or she is. Overblown praise is usually followed closely by its companion, heavy-duty arm-twisting. "Mary, you decorate cakes more exquisitely than anyone in the entire universe! Would you teach the primary girls Sunday school class?" Most of us have learned the truth of the proverb about the self-serving flatterer: "Whoever flatters his neighbor is spreading a net at his feet." (Proverbs 29:5 NIV)

Counterfeit practices of honor detract from the genuine honor that is due others. Paul advised the Philippians, "Do nothing out of selfish ambition or vain conceit, but in humility consider others better than yourselves." (Philippians 2:3 NIV) The example of Jesus which follows, demonstrates an attitude of love which serves others rather than seeks to be served.

It is the nature of love to hold others in tender regard, to rejoice in the good in them, to see the potential in them. And we can learn many genuine ways of expressing respect born of love. To say that we must be cautious about flattery does not mean that we should be stingy with praise and encouragement. An honoring love appreciates and draws out the best in others, but it can do it best by avoiding hypocrisy and the lies of exaggeration. So, exalted readers, let's learn genuinely to honor one another.

The All-Rounder

The Orvis catalog, a favorite among the flood of catalogs that mysteriously appear in our mailbox, is almost no problem at all to me. I can pass by the fatwood kindling and Harris tweed sports coats without suffering even a slight elevation of pulse rate. But the page displaying the four-piece "All-Rounder" graphite fly rod quickens my heartbeat every time. The inner accountant immediately objects, "You can't spend that kind of money on a fishing pole!" (Intentionally rejecting the more elegant term "fly rod.") "Yeah, especially with so many needy people in the world!" the moralist chimes in.

The inner war is on. The bug-eyed self so taken by terms like "Orvis," "graphite," or "favorite of Western fishing guides" is so shamefully eager to own this rod that the rationalizing self must stand in the gap. "It may be expensive, but it really is practical. So versatile. Probably the last rod you would ever need to buy. Besides, the pleasure it would provide would surely enhance your health and productivity." Other inner voices do not retreat in the face of such smooth persuasion, so skirmishes continue until a truce (often temporary) is called.

Inner battles over fishing rods may seem ludicrous to those whose temptations fall more toward clothes or cars, stereos or knick-knacks. I suspect they are more than ludicrous. More likely they are dangerous, because such struggles stir up discontent and divert our devotion to God.

If the All-Rounder skirmish is mine alone, the larger battle is not. The urge to own wages guerilla warfare with many of us. Mounting hit-and-run attacks in unexpected times and places, it surprises us and keeps us off-balance. It challenges a proper sense of what is sufficient and tricks us, however briefly, into seeing what we own as the source of joy.

A friend who had just moved complained, "I can't believe how much stuff we have!" I, too, have blushed a bit when we have had to load our hoard into a U-Haul truck. Perhaps danger lurks less, however, in how much we have than in how much we want.

Even in greed there is subtlety. Every sensible person recognizes blatant materialism in the desire for many things and rejects it out of hand. But the words "If I just had/could do X, then I would be content" more easily deceive us because we overlook the fact that the formula never disappears. "X" merely changes. The "one more thing" temptation is subtler, then, because it draws us into desiring many things one at a time. Such an obsession, however small its object, is large enough to cripple us inwardly.

Diagnosis is easier than a cure, especially in a society that considers compulsive greed a normal and noble human trait. Anyone who has tried to live in Christian simplicity can witness to the difficulty of learning a better way. An important part of a cure, however, lies in how we focus our attention. Give less attention to what sparks desire and discontent. Focus instead on God and God's goodness.

Perhaps other people are invulnerable to the seeds of desire planted by window-shopping, browsing though catalogs ("wish books" my family called them), reading sales flyers, seeing innumerable television ads, or driving through wealthy neighborhoods to ogle the scope and design of their homes and grounds. I'm not. The more I give my attention, even innocently, to such things, the more easily scatteredness and numbnesss displace inner peace.

To focus instead on God takes a simple, positive step toward meeting a complex problem. To recognize and give thanks for God's provision and love, for example, is a powerful antidote to the poison of obsessive desire. So is to make our greatest obsession to know and love God. Jesus' teaching that one cannot love both God and money does have a wonderful backhand. If we do indeed love God with all of our being, greed cannot long grip us. It is a step this simple that leads to restful freedom.

Peter and John abandoned nets and boats to follow Jesus, an act that makes the All-Rounder skirmish look pretty silly. After all, those who would follow Christ in any age must yearn for that alone.

Beds of Ease

"Idling about on beds of ease wishing for something fancier, they stole from the bedless poor everything but their underwear. Rising well rested (and slightly hung over), they went to sing praise to God for choosing them and providing such bounty."

The jarring words of the prophet at the church door seemed exaggerated and treasonous, full of violence and ruin. They seemed so to the prophet, too, but they were the only words he had, for he saw the world through God's eyes and not through the colored lenses of his nation's flag. He would have preferred silence, but discovered that the fire of love which God enkindled in his heart was also a fire burning in his bones that seared silence, consumed complacency, and demanded unflagging obedience to the divine command alone.

To risk seeing the world through God's eyes always threatens to put us at odds with the status quo, for God does not guarantee to see things as our culture sees them, as we have traditionally seen them, or as we would like to see them. Once the love of God is rooted deeply in our hearts, we begin to share the divine compassion for the world, a compassion that emerges in both tenderness and judgment.

Having known the love of God, can we do less than experience deep horror at the intentional slaughter of innocents in Lebanon and the United States' complicity in it? Can our hearts be hardened to families whose members have been spirited away by murderous governments in Central America? Can we fail to plead for the disadvantaged instead of hiding, even boldly, behind Jesus' phrase, "the poor are with you always," and labeling them all "welfare cheats?" The Bible witnesses clearly that God cannot abide callousness and carnage, for they violate God's loving purposes for all of creation. The issues may vary, but the compassion of God remains the same.

If we know the heart of God, we like the prophets, must tell the truth: God will not long endure a nation which uses the divine name to hallow its plans for limited nuclear wars, its oppression and neglect of the poor, its greed and its vanity. Nor will God long embrace "Children of Light" who dally with such darkness until its shadow dims and even extinguishes their beacon altogether.

The love of God also requires us to live the truth. We cannot talk peace at the meetinghouse and vote war at the polls. We cannot laud self-sacrifice and generosity in Sunday School and applaud the politics and economics of greed at the office. If Christian commitment and the real world intersect at all, then the people of God must actively cultivate justice, the care of the needy, and the healing of individuals and of the structures of society. God surely will require of each one a different role, but in no case will obedience demand idle complacency.

This is hardly a call for political or social action for its own sake, but for faithful service that proceeds out of the intimate knowledge of God. Too often Friends have acted in a spirit of human wisdom and partisan politics, completely uninformed by prayer and by the power of God. Such activity has often failed and even damaged the cause of right. Without prayer, it deserves to fail.

On the other hand, there is a type of prayer and prattle of praise that revolts God. To self-righteous Israel came the word, "Let me have no more of the din of your chanting, no more of your strumming on harps. But let justice flow like water and integrity like an unfailing stream." (Amos 5:23–24 JB) Piety and politics cannot be separated. Devotion to God must penetrate every detail of daily living. Anything less fails to understand the meaning of the Gospel.

It has long embarrassed me to think that Friends ever held other human beings as slaves, though they did, all the while comfortably "doing good and doing well." Change came only when John Woolman (and others) challenged them, cherishing absolute devotion to God more than the security of the status quo. In this time when Christianity is being pirated away by the spirit of our culture, we, too, need a people of God who know that faithfulness involves all of life, who will rise from their beds of ease and who will walk courageously in the ways of God. Let's be such a people.

Good News and Peace

The Christian tasks of peace and evangelism often are set at odds with one another. For example, the rejection of discussions of peace by planners of a world conference on evangelism led to the beginning of the New Call to Peacemaking. When Billy Graham announced his disapproval of nuclear weapons, American Christianity was startled. Surely this was not the business of a prominent evangelist! Even among Friends tension between these two concerns is often found. Many local and yearly meetings have identifiable sub-groups of peace people and evangelistic people. Sometimes they even fight each other.

Recognizing this traditional difficulty, Iowa Yearly Meeting held a conference on "The Quaker Heritage: Peace and Evangelism" in 1980. The presentations and discussions during the weekend workshop pointed out again the importance of resolving the tension. Peace and evangelism belong together. To keep them together may affect both our basic understandings and our methods.

To understand clearly, one must see that peace is not peripheral to the Gospel. In fact, it is so important that the New Testament often uses the phrase "the gospel of peace." At the heart of the Christian message is Jesus Christ who is the best peacemaker (or reconciler) of all. This message undeniably includes the call to repentance, the forgiveness of sins, and the reconciliation of individuals to God. However, Christ was also God's way of reconciling the whole world— the whole creation. Jesus made peace by his death on the cross. (2 Corinthians 5:19; Colossians 1:20)

Not only did Jesus make peace through his own obedience to God, he also called his disciples to live peaceably and to be peacemakers. True repentance includes the resolve to follow Christ in all that he taught, including the practice of peace.

It is the combination of personal renewal in Christ and obedience to Christ's commands that gives such strength to George Fox's classic statement in refusing to gain his freedom from prison by becoming an army captain: "I told them I lived in the virtue of that life and power that took away the occasion of all wars. . . . I told them I was come into the covenant of peace which was before wars and strifes were." (Nickalls, *Journal*, p.65)

Holding peace and evangelism together should also affect our methods. For example, those who evangelize (by whatever means) must not be satisfied with an appeal that merely calls people to save their own skins. Evangelists must call people not only to be liberated from sin but also to be enslaved to Christ. Part of evangelism must be training in enduring discipleship, "teaching them to observe all that I commanded." (Matthew 28:20 RSV) Evangelizing for discipleship includes evangelizing for peace.

Meanwhile, those actively serving peace must recognize that it is the transforming power of God in Christ that makes peace possible, even though a variety of methods and structures may create favorable conditions for peace. We cannot call for peaceful living and at the same time belittle repentance. Indeed, part of the work of peacemaking must be to call individuals and groups away from their pride, greed, and misguided sense of self-sufficiency. Peacemaking includes calling people to resolve their war with God.

The world is dying—perhaps killing itself—for lack of a whole Gospel. If Friends have a message for this age, it must be the complete story—peace with God and peace on earth. In such desperate times only this can truly be Good News.

Hospitable Friends

Recently, after we had entertained visiting Friends overnight on several occasions, one of our neighbors asked, "Does your church tell you that you have to do that?" My wife, Margi, responded, "No, these are our friends. We like to do it." It had not occurred to me up to that point that showing hospitality was unusual, even though I especially enjoy being either a host or a guest.

Hospitality has been a wonderful quality of Friends through the years. In a time when hospitality is threatened, it can continue to characterize Friends today.

Early Friends were strengthened immeasurably by the openhanded hospitality of the Fells of Swarthmore Hall. That spirit traveled at least from northwest England to the northeastern United States. Rufus Jones, in recalling his boyhood in Maine, describes how at the rise of the meeting for business "began the invasion of the homes in the neighborhood. Every dining-room had its long table, and an elastic supply to fit the rather reckless invitation which all the members of the family gave with little or no consultation." For Jones, memories of the blend of "positive religion and genuine hospitality" endured for a lifetime.

Fortunately, hospitality has not become as rare as Quaker gray. Many Friends gladly open their homes to others for meals or to traveling Friends for lodging. Some continue to prepare more food than is necessary for their families alone so that they can invite visitors or other Friends home with them after meeting for worship. Others in college communities faithfully invite students for meals or simple social occasions.

Despite the joyful benefits of hospitality and its value in building the community of faith, it seems threatened in our time. Unhappily, some Friends are too busy pursuing their own interests to take time for it. The stunning reputations of hospitality wizards intimidate others. Still others have limited means and feel that what they could offer would be inadequate. Yet hospitality must continue.

Some offer hospitality more easily than others due to both means and aptitude. This does not surprise us. Yet Paul apparently urges all Christians to practice hospitality (Romans 12:13), and 1 Peter 4:9 pointedly advises, "Welcome each other into your houses without grumbling." (JB) All of us need to seek occasions to share our lives with others in this way.

If our personal schedules prevent us from offering hospitality, it is time to simplify our schedules. If we are too busy to share our lives with others, we are too busy.

Friends need not entertain to impress others, nor do they need to be embarrassed that others can entertain more lavishly than they. Hospitality can (and should) be offered simply and within one's means. A plaque in the home of some very gracious Friends includes these words: "Let the guest sojourning here know that in this home our life is simple. What we cannot afford we do not offer, but what good cheer we can give, we give gladly."

Hospitality is simply offering our love and our lives to others as freely and as sincerely as possible. It does not seek reward or praise, but has its own reward in joy. It is a privilege that no Friend should fail to exercise.

By the way, when you next visit Wichita (now Newberg, Oregon), why don't you stop in for dinner?

The Binoculared Ones

Careful occasional observation has persuaded me that there are more birdwatchers per thousand (bpt) among Friends than among many other Christians. Just why Quakers may have a higher bpt ratio than Presbyterians or Slavonic Baptists puzzles me. However, despite my overexposure to this Friendly binoculared breed, I think it is true.

There is a long tradition of interest in the natural sciences among Friends. Margaret H. Bacon in *The Quiet Rebels* points out that William Bartram is thought of as the first American ornithologist and his father John as America's first botanist. A well-known Quaker paleontologist of the last century, Edward Drinker Cope, was the one who discovered the dinosaur fossils of the American West. A Cope of this century, James, of Earlham College, is probably singlehandedly responsible for thousands of Friendly birdwatchers.

To these names others could be added, but that still would not answer the questions of why our bpt ratio is so high. Some have answered that Quakers weren't allowed to have real fun so settled for the study and appreciation of the natural world. This answer will probably satisfy those who know only four species of American birds—small, medium, large, and robins.

The "substitute for fun" argument, however, even if it has a grain of truth, widely misses the mark. We come closer when we remember that Quakers see all of life as an arena for God's presence and action. The natural world was created and is sustained by God. It witnesses to God. All truth, whether "religious" or "scientific," is part of God's truth. Taking God seriously in all of life made them cherish the world, and this insight still helps.

To take the world seriously can remind us of the graciousness and grandeur of God. Though this seems obvious, we must not underestimate its importance for our time. In the face of technological and falsely scientific arrogance, to know the world intimately can renew a sense of wonder. In the face of simplistic, religion-in-a-box Christianity, to watch the world with our hearts open can restore the sense of otherness, our awareness that God bursts our boxes.

If we learn truly to observe and appreciate the world, it can deliver us from the frantic pace of our age. Nature does not yield the depth of its wonder, its beauty, its truth to the quick glance. We can be in the world without seeing or savoring it. Among those who miss "the great out-of-doors" are those who dash madly from one national park to another in order to add each site to the trophy list of "places I've been." Another example of those who miss the world is fishermen who invade lakes and streams only to catch, weigh, measure, count and keep every fish legally possible.

Both of these examples are responses to the question, "What did you do? What did you accomplish?" It is a sensible question raised with insensible force in our society. We can be delivered from its tyranny if we learn to observe and appreciate the world, if we see ourselves as part of the world rather than see the world as merely a platform for human activity. If we can learn to stop in wonder, we can also stop our frantic pace.

To know the world also rebukes our exaggerated concern for utility, found in the question, "What is it good for?" A cherished fishing buddy, Wally McClung, taught me a lot about this. While driving to the mighty Deschutes River ("The fish are biting," I was thinking), he stopped by the side of the road and walked with me in tow several hundred yards to show me a flower. It was a tiny, orchid-like flower that grows in a limited range near Mt. Hood and lives only a very short time in the early spring. It probably isn't good for anything. But I'm sure God delighted in it as in the rest of creation in saying, "That's good. That's very good!" I delighted too, and learned again that "What's it good for?" is not always a useful question.

Perhaps you are not inclined to join the binoculared ones. All of us however, can learn more about our own lives, about God and God's truth by coming to cherish our world. Summer will soon slip away and fall greet us with its glory. May we be sensitive enough to our world to be filled with wonder and delight. Then we may say, "Thanks, God, that really is very good!"

Fixing Education

Recently two reports sharply critical of American education have prompted quibbling speeches from many quarters: indignant oratory from politicians who promise to fix it, worried accusations from parents who fear their children are destined for illiteracy, defensive cries from some educators who insist that warnings of a "nation at risk" exaggerate the problem. All agree, however, that there is a problem and many propose solutions.

The most popular analyses suggest that our problems in education can be solved with basically technocratic solutions—higher standards, higher salaries, longer school days, better techniques and so on. Some of these approaches might shrink the problems a bit. However, I suggest (even without statistical proof) that many of the problems in education have a deeper root in the spiritual malaise of our society. At this level the educational decline will not yield to a technocratic fix. Only the impact of spiritual insight can move us forward.

The people of God can help in a unique way in this time by identifying the cancers of the spirit that sap energy and by actively fighting them both publicly and privately.

Two of the most destructive elements of our modern malaise, for example, are uncertainty about the future and uncertainty about one's own identity and importance. The scenarios of military, economic and environmental disaster are a constant undercurrent in contemporary life. If there is a future, we wonder, is it worth having? Similarly, any sense of personal worth is sharply challenged. The immensity of the universe and the giant scale of the structures of society often create a sense of powerlessness and insignificance. Feelings of self-worth are further threatened by widespread teaching that humans are merely creatures of accident, shaped principally by impersonal chemical, genetic and environmental forces.

Other factors join with these to produce a crisis of the spirit that emerges in melancholy or pessimism, in living principally for the present and for personal satisfaction. The key words become "me" and "now." The way of life becomes the plaintive Peggy Lee refrain—"If that's all there is, then let's keep dancing, let's break out the booze and have a ball."

It should surprise us very little that motivation for learning (and for significant teaching) may be on the wane. Nor is it unexpected that those who do want to learn seem more eager to be certified for high-dollar jobs than to prepare to serve others or to try to change the world for good. The "success" route pays off doubly by providing resources for instant personal pleasure and by providing a kind of hollow dignity accorded by our society to the rich. In the end, perhaps we should say that many modern students simply don't have the heart to learn.

Technofix will not even touch this wound of the spirit. It may dazzle and distract. It might even patch the gaping sore. But it will not heal it.

On the other hand, Christians have Good News to meet this deep malaise. It is news of health and wholeness. The news is that each individual is infinitely important to the One who sustains the vast universe. It is that God refuses to give up on the world and is eager to bring the loving, divine purpose to fulfillment. The Good News is that God's power still overreaches the powers of this evil age. Against great odds, Christ's victory is typically won through the small, the despised and the unexpected. The eyes of faith see that the Lamb's victory is winning its way even now with subtlety and surprise. Good news! God delights in every creature. God yearns for the world to be whole. God reigns in power.

If people are to learn and live well in this dark age, they need the bright message of God's love and power. Through us they can have it. We ourselves may struggle to hold and to be held by the truth that there really is Good News. Yet as we are gripped by it, we must find creative, winsome ways to let it penetrate our world. This has been and is still our call.

Light for Learning

Just as one needs steps to take toward a cure when he/she is sick, so the diagnosis in our column on "Fixing Education" is incomplete without a prescription for action. The common uncertainty about the future and about one's own worth can be met, we suggested, by the Christian message of God's concern and tenderness toward all of creation and the presence among us of God in power. Fortunately, these insights can be translated into effective action in our educational world. Friends have often led the way in this task and they can again. What action, then, can we take?

The principal responsibility for teaching the Christian ideas that rescue us from the selfish melancholy of the age still lies in the home and in the church. Parents must consciously tend to the teaching task, nurturing their own lives to be examples that "adorn Truth" (as Fox put it) as well as seeking both casual and structured times for instruction at home. Meetings, too, must watch over their example and teaching so that their members will grow strong and have the vision to make a difference in the world. More than refuges, our homes and meetings need to be boot camps training us all for the Lamb's War.

Beyond homes and meetings, Friends schools at all levels can contribute substantially through applying freshly the best of our vision of education. What does it mean now to treasure integrity, community, simplicity, the life of worship, the importance of each individual and other traditional values? One Friends college has demonstrated the kind of thoughtfulness we need by refusing to fall in blindly with the stampede to offer a computer major. Instead of being merely opportunistic, the college leaders have delayed in order to consider carefully the social and ethical implications of this new technology and how it would be appropriate to teach it in the context of Friends values. Friends schools can be islands of hope and sanity in a world gone mad if they let Truth penetrate every aspect of their common life and if they guard against capitulating thoughtlessly to our culture.

Through observation and interest, Friends can also raise the level of public education. Even a few people who are thoughtful and actively involved can substantially influence public schools. Opportunities for involvement abound—personal conferences with teachers and administrators, parent-teacher organizations, expressions of concern to school boards and, of course, encouragement for Christian teachers whose leavening influence can profoundly shape the life of a school.

We should hardly expect that public schools will become hothouses for Christian values. They won't. But we can insist that they not be hostile to such values and, even better, that some of the best of our vision be reflected in the life of the school. For example, we should insist that the process of education should be just and should guard each individual's worth. Procedures should not be arbitrary, discriminatory or dehumanizing. Teachers should not be allowed the privilege of demeaning children (or each other) through verbal abuse or other means.

Similarly we can show an active interest in curriculum. We can insist that teaching highlight the noblest and best of the human endeavor. Through literature, the arts and the thoughtful reflections of many disciplines students can come to see outwardly the potential that echoes inwardly. This in itself is not sufficient but it is lifting to be exposed to the moments when we have approximated the best that we can be.

Perhaps these few suggestions about how to bring light to learning can help others begin to take specific action. Yet how much better it would be if Friends everywhere would dream of ways to influence for Truth's sake the teachers and schools in their own communities. In this way, too, we can shine like beacons in our world.

Shall Pac-Man be Praised?

The age of electronic games has (unmercifully) arrived, and is now surrounding us with crunching, pinging, and points of colored light exploding across TV screens. I'm almost accustomed to being accosted at every turn by Pac-Man, Defenders, and their silicon-chip king. But the blips and beeps that answer the sound of dropping quarters raise old questions with new force: what purpose do recreation and leisure serve? Which amusements or activities best serve that purpose?

Friends have long recognized the usefulness of leisure and recreation in restoring our physical and spiritual health, in adjusting our perspective on life, and in increasing our joy in living. These are wonderful gifts from God, who also knows of laughter and sport and rest. The question, then, that comes to us is not whether recreation is okay, but which activities to choose. Contemporary society urges on us an ever-expanding array of recreational choices—sports, crafts, music, theater, travel, nature activities, and much more. Some activities will serve us better than others, so we need to be wise in choosing. After all, our recreation, like all of life, is part of our devotion to God.

A query from Philadelphia Yearly Meeting's *Faith and Practice* (1972) both suggests an approach and gives specific counsel: "Do you choose recreations which will strengthen the physical, mental, and spiritual life of yourself and your family, and do you avoid those that may be a hindrance to you and to others?" This is a searching question, one that could become a wise and friendly guide.

Other questions may also help. For example: "Is this activity consistent with the wise and responsible use of my time, energy and resources?" As New England Friends note in their *Faith and Practice*, recreational activities should not dominate one's life, demanding more of our time or money than is appropriate. Yet in any hobby wise stewardship may easily be forgotten. Photographers collect lenses, filters, and gadgets of all sorts. Fishermen are tempted perpetually by a better rod (this year it's boron), a craftier lure, and bigger boxes in which to put their accumulated treasures. Some are so enchanted by the out-of-doors—camping, skiing, hiking—that they rarely find their way to worship with other Christians when their sport is in season. Each activity has its own temptations to excess. Yet Christian responsibility requires that nothing claim a disproportionate part of our lives.

"Does this activity increase life or diminish life? Does it restore or destroy?" Some types of recreation rejuvenate the body and help recharge the spirit. Others dissipate our physical energies and diminish our spiritual vitality. We feel a dull emptiness or cheapening for having participated in them. Recreation helps shape who we are, so we would be wise to judge whether our activities build us up or tear us down.

"Does this activity express the image of God in me?" Among the other things, does it allow me to be a whole person and to relate to others in love? Does it encourage the expression of the immense God-given capacity to create? Our activities should not demean us but should instead allow the image of God in humankind to be showcased.

"Does this activity honor God? Does it direct me back to God in praise?" From tennis to gardening, from cooking to singing, all of this can be done in a way that honors God and allows us to discover in it a spirit of praise. Activities which restrict in any way our wholehearted delight in God should be shunned. The rest can be undertaken with great gladness.

Leisure and recreation are wonderful gifts of God. Through wise choice, and for our good, let's learn to receive them with joy.

Hearing **Scripture**

Tasty Torah

A graphic flyer showing a clown tipping his hat informs us:
"THIS LIFE IS A TEST.

IT IS ONLY A TEST.

HAD THIS BEEN AN ACTUAL LIFE, YOU WOULD HAVE BEEN GIVEN FURTHER INSTRUCTIONS ON WHERE TO GO AND WHAT TO DO."

It's a sober note whose humor depends on a lot of people feeling like it's too true.

Yet, in sharp contrast to this emptiness, the Old Testament singers bubble over with enthusiasm that they have, in fact, been given further instructions for an actual life. Psalms 19 and 119 are especially extravagant. God's instructions for life are a lamp to the feet, a light to the path. Through them God gives understanding to even "simple" folk. These singers "delight" in God's instructions—they long for them, rejoice in them, love and treasure them, meditate on and observe them. Better yet, they're better than money, even lots of it. They're sweeter than honey, or as Eugene Peterson paraphrases it in *The Message*, "better than red ripe strawberries in spring." Indeed, the truly happy person is one who (Peterson again) "thrills" to God's instructions and "chews" on them constantly. (Psalm 1)

Such bursts of delight may puzzle modern readers, especially when they remember that this enthusiasm is for "Torah," usually translated "Law." What are we to make of this beyond lingering adolescent suspicions that God sets up rules to keep anyone from having a good time? And it won't do to suppose these Israelite singers were too stupid to know how oppressed they were. Let me suggest three barriers that may keep us from understanding, even sharing, their joy.

Bluntly, one barrier might be that we don't like "rules" of any sort. A lot of folk just want to do whatever they please, though it's not a new approach. The Old Testament talks repeatedly about the folly of those who want to do whatever seems good in their own opinion ("in their own eyes"). Torah doesn't thrill folk who know better than God.

Another barrier may be that we have too narrow an understanding of Torah, seeing it more as a realm of laws and judges than one of teaching and guidance. Certainly the Old Testament includes many civil and ritual laws (which, of course, pose challenges for modern interpreters), but Torah breaks out of the limits of law codes. The root of the word "Torah" and the ways the Israelites speak of God's kindness in giving it strongly suggest the practical guidance that came through worship, prayer, priests and prophets, proverbs, and much more.

A third block may be that Christians may fail to see the continuing value of these life instructions. Certainly the Gospel frees us from legalistic abuses of the "Law." Yet, Jesus preserved continuity by saying pointedly that he hadn't come to do away with Torah but to fulfill it. He teaches, as does the Church after him, that loving God and neighbor gather up the Law and the Prophets. Yet Jesus and the Apostles don't leave these as grand but vague principles. They don't hesitate at all to give us clear pictures of what acting in love looks like. These laws of love under God's guidance still give us practical instructions for living a real life.

We'd do well to listen gladly to extravagant songs about Torah. God's gracious instructions spread a sumptuous table. We can dive in, chew on Torah, and lick our chops. We might even join in a boisterous chorus of "Tasty Torah, sweeter than honey, better than strawberries and cream."

The Heavens Are Falling

As James Thurber recounts it, there was once a little red hen who, having felt something fall on her head, ran about the barnyard shouting, "The heavens are falling down!" much to the amusement of the other creatures. Yet even as they laughed and lampooned, "Suddenly with an awful roar great chunks of crystallized cloud and huge blocks of icy blue sky began to drop on everybody from above, and everybody was killed ... for the heavens actually *were* falling down." Thurber's moral? "It wouldn't surprise me a bit if they did."(*Fables for Our Time*, p. 71)

We're not short on warnings ourselves. Whether it's Ms. Hen and Associates or pronouncements from the Department of Dire Warnings (DDW), lots of folks are glad to tell us the sky is falling: professional fear-mongers, neighbors and friends, talk show hosts, advertisers, the Heavens-Falling Division of DDW.

Sometimes the heavens actually are falling. Relationships fall apart, finances go south, good health disappears, leaders speak power to truth, and trusted social structures seem to go to the nether regions in a handbasket. And we sit, dazed and devastated, surrounded by chunks of sky, or in Martin Luther's hymn paraphrase, by a "flood of mortal ills."

The poets of Psalm 46 sing at the prospect of precisely such a disaster: "Though the earth give way, and the mountains fall into the heart of the sea." (v. 2) From a Hebrew viewpoint, "The heavens are falling." The world is in chaos and enemies are at the gate. Yet they sang, "God is our refuge and strength, an ever-present help in trouble. Therefore we will not fear . . ." (vv. 1–2 NIV)

Why not? Delusional fears are one thing, but real calamity is quite another. Fear makes sense, unless we know what the psalmists know. God is ever-present (or "ever-ready") to help in the face of trouble. The singers call on two powerful images from Israel's faith, both of which point to God's great power and loving purposes.

The first image pictures the great fortress city that is God's dwelling place, the seat of God's universal reign. At the center of the world and above all other mountains (see Isaiah 2), its Eden-like waters flow to give security against siege warfare, but also to give life to all that it touches. (We see this river again in Ezekiel 47 and Revelation 22 where abundance springs up constantly by its banks.) And the God who dwells in this city can melt creation with a shout as easily as establish it with a word.

The second image thrills to the marvel of God ending wars all over the world and piling their weapons on a bonfire. Certainly not all wars then or now have ended, yet God does end wars. Even more, God shares with us our longing for life and wholeness, *shalom* at its fullest, and has the will and the power to carry it out. For this reason, we can know that no disaster can overmatch God's power, no calamity can outstrip God's love. George Fox knew this, too, in his confidence that "the power of the Lord is over all" and that "an infinite ocean of light and love flow[s] over the ocean of darkness and death."

So when our worlds are falling apart, in the face of puzzlement and pain, the psalmists urge, "Be still." (Psalm 46:10 NIV) Pause a while. Step back. Take a deep breath. Don't panic. Don't conjure up frantic contingency plans. Don't alarm the whole barnyard. Remember who you're dealing with. Let God be God, "a bulwark never failing." Trust that the God over all is with us among the icy chunks. Lean into God. Be still.

Anointed or Just Greasy?

The king's handlers surely struggled some days to prepare the king to go to worship. On the days he only had to show up they'd tell him to stay focused, to be sure not to gawk around and act distracted. But preparing him to speak or sing gave them fits. Projecting courage and conviction, the king had to say he was living right, doing justice, rejecting crooks and evil-doers, and throwing all the liars out of his administration. (Psalm 101) The Old Testament prophets and historians pointedly report that a lot of Israel's kings didn't live up to their songs in worship. So no doubt it was hard to teach them to sing sincerely, without smirks, giggles, or sly winks.

Israel knew what good kings looked like. They wanted, and knew God wants, leaders who are fair, truthful, wise, compassionate and especially watching out for the interests of the most vulnerable people in society—the widows and orphans, the poor and "strangers." (for example, Isaiah 9:6–7, 11:1–5) We share their hope and share their disappointment when leaders ignore these ideals while cozying up to their buddies and choosing to serve themselves. The vulnerable ones always suffer most.

Of course, the Judeans didn't get to choose God's "Anointed," as the Davidic king was routinely called. Nor did the early Christians have a lot of say about who would be the next Caesar, though more than a few died for refusing to bend the knee to him as "God." But I get to vote. So I try to think how I can help choose leaders and public policies that would move toward God's ideal.

It's easy to get cynical at this point. Some folks say that all politicians are liars so you just choose the liars you like. Maybe you like their style or looks or sound bites on a favorite issue. Or maybe you always vote Demopublican or flip a coin. I hope and think that we can do better than this but often discover how easily I can get waylaid by dismay, frustration, even anger.

Just when stewing in frustration seems like a fine moral choice, what God wants in the world bounces back at me. The once-and-for-all "Anointed One" has come, has defeated the powers, and reigns as Lord. The Peaceable Kingdom has begun, and, by who they are, all who choose to be citizens of that Kingdom are to extend its power and principles into every sphere of influence that they have. We can actively shape our homes, our relationships, our congregations, our communities, our businesses, schools, and workplaces.

Truth, justice, compassion, and protecting the poor are not merely God's principles, they are God's passion. God requires them, yes, but also delights in them. Those who share God's delight find practical ways to shape their world. I think of Benny who as a school principal found creative ways to serve kids and their families in the poorest part of town. Or Wallen who cautioned a banker that foreclosing on a recent widow's house might be legal but wasn't right. Or Friends who together mounted a court watching project to discover how vulnerable defendants might be more justly served. Or Colin who started a youth soccer program to help overcome tensions in an ethnically diverse community. To these each of us can add what others have done or what we might do (even when we vote) to live out God's passion in our worlds.

Corrupt kings and cocky Caesars don't have the power they, and sometimes we, think. They are only God's finger-snap away from being brought down. (Maybe we can help.) Whatever our apparent circumstances, however, we can gladly serve the One who rules over all, whose power has no limit, whose love has no end, and whose delight brings joy to the world.

Glad for Today

For several months now I've been reading, probably with you, brief biographical sketches of individuals who died at the World Trade Center last September 11, 2001. For each one, scarcely 150 words describe their dreams, personalities, relationships, the ways they loved to spend their time. These snapshots of lives lived, and their abrupt end, touch us and raise questions. Some of our questions explore fear and our desire for security and control, but many push us to ask again what makes life worth living.

My reflections on this keep circling back to the Book of Ecclesiastes (Qoheleth). Mixed with all of its challenges to interpreters, it offers timely insights. The short form is this: Today is important. It's a gift. Live it with joy and thankfulness.

What folks regard as "dark" in Ecclesiastes largely is a rejection of what we often think makes life worth living. Some of us bristle when "Qoheleth" ("the Preacher") undercuts the idea that we can leave a "legacy." Whatever name you make for yourself, he says, will soon be forgotten. Others are equally put off by his discounting the value of making a fortune, doing "great things," immersing ourselves in pleasure, or, in some measure, gaining great "wisdom." Ecclesiastes, however, is not simply a tract against lifestyles of the rich and famous. It's a cautionary word to folks then and now who compulsively seek to garnish their reputation, guarantee their financial security, and control at least their little piece of the world.

Qoheleth cautions us, first of all, that life is fragile. September 11 was a massive reminder of that, though, if we pay attention, we all can see such fragility in our ordinary experience. The Old Testament often alludes to human life as being like the morning fog that quickly burns off, or the dew on the grass the sun suddenly dries, or new sprouts of grass in the desert that the hot east wind flattens. Ecclesiastes makes the same point with the word that is misleadingly translated "vanity" or "meaningless." Without reviewing the history of translation here, we can simply note that the Hebrew word behind it tries to convey fragility. Life is like a vapor, a puff of wind. It's fleeting and can quickly confound our plans, our securities, our efforts to guarantee what is yet to come.

At the same time, Ecclesiastes reminds us that life is God's gift to us. What we eat and drink, the work that we do, the comforts we enjoy, and the dear relationships we cherish all come from God.

Seeing life as a fragile gift leads to the point Ecclesiastes makes repeatedly. (See 2:24–25; 3:12–13, 22; 5:17; 8:15; 9:7–8) Live each day, he says, with joy, gladness, and gratitude. Give up the striving and scheming that are not only futile but also steal the present. Live in joy now. "This is the day the Lord has made; let us rejoice and be glad in it." (Psalm 118:24 NIV)

Lest we're inclined to take this counsel lightly because we think of Qoheleth as grumpy, we should note that Jesus adds his voice in the Sermon on the Mount. "Therefore I tell you, do not worry about your life…" God cares generously for the birds, the lilies, the grass of the field and will even more gladly care for you. So "do not worry about tomorrow, for tomorrow will worry about itself. Each day has enough trouble of its own." (Matthew 6:25–34 NIV)

This day, and every day, is an important day. It's the one God has given us. Let's eat and drink gladly, enjoy our work, love our families. Let's live it with joy and thankfulness.

Watching Our Lips Move

You probably know the formula joke: "How can you tell when (fill in the blank) is lying? His lips are moving." (Discerning women will be delighted that I have used the almost generic "he" here.) Working in the Psalms recently reminded me how often we use the language of "lips" to talk about right living. We have loose lips and tight lips, flattering lips, honest and deceitful lips. If you lip off or give someone lip you could wind up with a fat lip or a split lip. Lips might drip with honey or have viper's poison on them. Lips can cause trouble or bomb or sink or synch. Now wonder the psalmist prayed, "Set a guard over my mouth, O Lord, keep watch over the door of my lips!" (Psalm 141:3 RSV) The topic of lips (with mouth and tongue) is so common in Psalms, Proverbs, and beyond that we'll not be just batting our gums to remind ourselves of the Bible's warnings.

Obviously the Bible praises "honest lips" and warns against "lying lips." Sometimes it associates "lying" with arrogant and contemptuous speech, not just getting the facts straight. (Psalms 31:18; 59:12) Quakers tell funny stories about being overly scrupulous with facts. One story recounts how one traveler observed to his Quaker companion that the sheep they saw in the field nearby had been shorn. The Friend agreed carefully, "Yes they have, on this side." I won't quarrel with careful truth-telling, but we may consider, too, that honesty may be more than the facts.

The historic practice of simple speech agrees with the biblical warning against flattery, which too often serves to manipulate. We can easily puff people up, whether with "honorific titles" or slathery compliments, for our own advantage. Some of us, at least, are suckers for the line, "Won't you help us with this? You are so good at it and we can hardly imagine being able to do it without you!" (Please forget I told you that.)

Fox himself targeted empty speech. They do not "possess what they profess, " he said, even as Jeremiah complained that God was always on the Israelites' lips, but "far from their hearts." (Jeremiah 12:2 NIV) Beyond ordinary hypocrisy, empty words include the high-sounding, heart-warming blather that has no content, that evades truth, that tries to distract and mislead. Between religious cliché and the carefully crafted political pandering of this election cycle, you can choose the illustrations you find most grievous.

The Bible also notes the danger of slander, which surely includes the careless labeling and name-calling that we can use too easily to dismiss each other. Sadly, a lot of public and private discourse has degenerated to mere attack language about "liberal" and "conservative" or right-, left-, or chicken- "winged" and more. Some of the labelers use simple, even crude words. Others seem fond of using a thesaurus to find fancy slanders. It hurts and obscures all the same. Truth and love both require us to find better ways to talk to and about one another.

The Letter of James observes what we all know—taming our speech is hard to do. Indeed, how we choose to talk directs how we live. (James 3) We never outgrow the prayer, "Set a guard over my mouth, O Lord, keep watch over the door of my lips!"

Prophets for Dummies

The growing number of "for-Dummies" books on my shelf recently startled me into self-assessment. Their yellow and black spines announce titles like *Word 6 for Dummies, Bird Watching for Dummies,* and *Brain Surgery for Dummies.* The books claim to be written by experts and they stick to basics. Lots of books complicate things: these keep it simple.

I thought maybe I would write a book *Prophets for Dummies,* since people like to complicate the prophets, too. But I think I can do the basics in a page, if I stretch it a bit.

Start with Micah 6:8: "[God has] already made it plain how to live, what to do…It's quite simple: Do what is fair and just to your neighbor, be compassionate and loyal in your love, and don't take yourself too seriously—take God seriously." (adapted from Peterson, *The Message*) Sometimes the Bible gives it to you compact, portable, explosive like that. (Compare also Isaiah 1:16–17; Jeremiah 9:23–24; Amos 5:24.)

Jesus, too, packed the Law and Prophets into a sentence: "Do to others as you would have them do to you." (Luke 6:31 NRSV) That's clear, which is not to say it's simple. (Even with clear instructions and precise diagrams, until you get the hang of it, you're likely to botch the first few brain surgeries.)

"Act justly." I'm convinced that many folks have no idea how passionately God wants justice. It's not about keeping rules; it's about loving people. The Bible presents picture after picture of what kind of society God wants. It's a place where no one gets ripped off at the store or railroaded in court or run roughshod over by their neighbors. It's a place where leaders look after the little people and not just their cronies, and, in some moving descriptions, where everyone, least to greatest, sits down to a great banquet in peace. I suspect we all want justice, at least for ourselves. Micah's simple complication is that we're supposed to want it for other people, too. In fact, God requires that we do all we can to see that they get it.

Peterson's paraphrase—"be compassionate and loyal in your love"—captures nicely most of what the elusive Hebrew word *hesed* is trying to say. We might only add, with Paul, "love never ends." (1 Corinthians 13:8 RSV) *Hesed* is a love that never quits. What would it mean for us to have unending compassion and loyal love for our neighbor, for the stranger, for our enemies, always seeking the very best for them? The prophets and Jesus give a lot of practical examples. It seems to me, however, that the principle is clear enough, even if it's going to take a lot of labs to quit botching it up.

"Walk humbly with your God" (the familiar translation) provides the key to the call to justice and love. It's not merely a pious footnote. "Walking humbly" moves us out of self-serving Center-of-the-Universe behaviors that corrupt justice and love. "Knowing" God intimately leads us to share God's passion for the world and its people (compare Jeremiah 9:24). It helps us to really pray, "Your will be done on earth," and to enter into its fulfillment. Serving justice and love out of arrogance and even self-sufficiency skews them both. Acts of justice and love born of humble obedience bring healing and joy.

Complicating the prophets further might obscure their message and make them easier to cope with. But sticking to these basics will help us to do what God wants.

Stand-Up Jesus

While studying humor in the Bible, one author surprised me by saying that Jesus did stand-up comedy. Even in all the years of singing the gospel song "Stand Up, Stand Up for Jesus," that had never occurred to me. But a lot of our great stand-up comics are Jewish, so I've been wondering what it would be like to imagine Jesus doing a Letterman or Seinfeld routine on the hills of Galilee.

"Hey, it's good to see you all today! I hear there are some folk here from Capernaum. [pause, cheers] Yeah, nice town, even with Pete's mother-in-law. [rim shot] Anybody from Nazareth? [pause] Guess not. Now *that* was a tough crowd! They nearly shoved me off a cliff! [laughter]

"How about a hand for my buddies, the Pharisees? [applause, maybe a jeer] They just got here from their prayers. [In stained-glass voice]: 'I thank you, Lord, that I'm not like those other guys.' [laughter] They've been giving me some great straight lines.

"You know, I kind of hate talking about other crowds, but that one the other day over on the next hill just didn't get it. I was joking with them about how they shouldn't let anything get in the way of the Kingdom—you know, cut off your hand, lop off your foot, and all. And then this guy who'd been staring way too hard at Mary nearly tore his eye out. Hey, just listen and laugh and do the right thing. We already have plenty of blind folks to help."

Now I don't think Jesus did stand-up comedy, quite. But he did tell funny stories and create comic word pictures. He exaggerated, bantered, teased, and cajoled. His parables show off all kinds of improbable characters (or maybe the way-too-probable people we already know)—the crooked judge and nagging widow (Luke 18:1–8), the neighbor leaning on the doorbell in the middle of the night and the sleepy crank who bails him out anyway (Luke 11:5–8), or the dishonest manager trying to bail himself out (Luke 16:1–9). Predating elephant jokes, Jesus told camel jokes—trying to thread a camel through the eye of a needle or, in trying to eat kosher, straining out gnats while choking down a camel. (I'll bet that would have worked, too, with trying to get a speck out of the other guy's eye while you have a camel in your own.) And when the Pharisees and Sadducees tried to trap him with "gotcha" games, Jesus' easy wins surely amazed and amused the crowds.

A friend reminded me recently of the ditty, "Quaker meeting has begun. No more laughing, no more fun." In view of such (even self-inflicted) slurs on our reputation, it pleases me that one of the earliest modern books that called attention to Jesus' playfulness is Elton Trueblood's *The Humor of Christ*. Elton argues, rightly, that we can't understand Jesus' teaching adequately when we fail to see his humor. Indeed, in some places getting the joke is the only way to catch on; it is the only way to take Jesus' message seriously. Humor teaches powerfully. It's a shame when we're so straight-laced that we don't get it.

Seeing Jesus' humor also can help us get to know Jesus better as genuinely joyful, warm, and friendly, as someone you would enjoy hanging out with. That makes a big difference for people who know Jesus mostly through word and visual images that depict Jesus only as sad, sorrowful, and scolding. Best of all, getting to know the joyful Jesus can draw us all more fully into the joy that Jesus is so eager to give us.

"Hey, did I tell you the one about the guy that got beat up on the way to Jericho . . . ?"

St. Fool

St. Paul was a fool. At least that's what he said when he wrote to the quarrelsome church at Corinth. They were playing "better-than-thee" over spiritual gifts and arguing about who followed the best leaders—Paul, Apollos or Peter. Maybe they colored the fight with hues of liberal or conservative, but they had the first spiritual trump party we know about, *"We just follow Christ."* (Follow 1 Corinthians 1–4 to see how Paul addresses these issues.)

To their credit, the Corinthians remind us how easy it is to start strutting our stuff and grabbing for bragging rights. But Paul tells them they have to get along. Besides, he says, bragging rights hardly fit a rag-tag bunch like them anyway.

Then Paul makes a bold move. He compares himself to the "fool" they all know in Greek theater, and it's not a pretty sight. The typical theater fool was a clown or mime who was often portrayed as not very smart, as ugly or deformed, who bumbled along as a speaker, was held in contempt socially, and, in the end, often got beat up. Paul teases and cajoles his readers with this, especially those so enamored with Apollos' eloquence and sophistication. He plays it to the hilt in chapter 4:8–13 when he says the Corinthians have become rich, kings even, honored, wise and strong while he, as the theater fools typically were, was brought on as a last minute spectacle for ridicule, was weak, hungry, and thirsty, badly clothed, tired and beaten, even sentenced to death. Not that they should feel ashamed over it all. (4:14) Paul's upside-down approach to these, his children in the faith, is both amusing and compelling.

Paul may well have fit the stereotype of fool in some ways. Maybe he really struggled to speak well, as he says, and it was only the work of the Spirit that got the message across. Perhaps he did indeed appear weak and unattractive. We know he embarrassed some of them by supporting himself with a low-class trade.

Paul the Fool's point about all the strutting and bragging is repeated and clear: God is who matters and gets things done. God triumphs through people and plans we'd never expect. God grows and brings harvest. God gives gifts. God is the source of new life. Any boasting needs to be about God.

Paul's quoting of Jeremiah here (Jeremiah 9:23–24) reminds us of where we go wrong. We tend to boast in the wisdom of new solutions and schemes, that we have terrific people and ample budgets together, that, according to the latest research, we know how to be effective. Jeremiah says to boast instead in knowing God, in living in loyalty and trust.

I think of Paul and this foolish abandon to God's love and power when we get cranky with each other. When we are tempted to label ourselves so everyone will know we are pure and true disciples, I want to remember that we're a rag-tag bunch, too, gathered and given life in God's mercy. When we quarrel over methods and strategies, as smart as we are and need to be, we must remember that it is God who gets things done, often outside all our plans. Maybe we could learn to be fools enough to get along.

Paul, fool that he was, also reminded us not to be too impressed with ourselves and not to be intimidated by not being impressive. After all, "God chose what is foolish in the world to shame the wise; God chose what is weak in the world to shame the strong; God chose what is low and despised in the world, things that are not, to reduce to nothing things that are, so that no one might boast in the presence of God." (1 Corinthians 1:27–29 NRSV) Instead, God intends that "with a demonstration of Spirit and of power, [our] faith might rest not on human wisdom but on the power of God." (1 Corinthians 2:4–5 NRSV)

Light Overcoming Darkness

Publishers of Fluff and Other Stuff

Ever since the Publishers of Truth began, Friends have been printing books and pamphlets. That fine tradition continues today with a variety of Quaker houses, both denominational and private. A great gap exists, however, in the Quaker publishing scene, and a new publishing firm is being formed to meet this market.

Friends have nothing for the average mass-market reader with a do-it-yourself or light-reading interest. Until now, no Quaker press has offered Friends books comparable to *Rebuild Your Piano in a Weekend* or *Laser Surgery for Fun and Profit*. This need is being met at last by POF Press whose first catalog reveals these titles:

The Quaker Alphabet Book. One of the signal achievements of ancient civilization was the invention of the alphabet. Its simplicity took literacy out of the hands of the elite and delivered it, in some measure, to the ordinary person. Over the years, however, Quakers have tried to restore the good old days of complexity by discovering how many configurations of the alphabet are possible while always including the letters F or Q. Hence these peculiar Quaker symbols: EFA, EFM, FGC, FUM, AFSC, FCNL, WQF, FWCC, FAHE, QUNO, YFNA, FY, YF, FCE, FUP, QRT, FTDG, ETC(F). This illustrated introductory book for adults initiates them into the Quaker alphabet mysteries succinctly and with a touch of humor.

How to Talk Quaker. This pocket-sized primer of the peculiarities of Friends vocabulary and speech forms should be particularly helpful to the novice and to persons who train seriously for bouts of "more Quaker than thee." The book includes treatments of terms like "concern" and "weight" as well as a guide to the modern uses of "thee" and "thou," from their value as signals of close friendship to their use as a curse ("you little thee-thou!"). The chapter on "Honest Ambiguity" gives indispensable counsel to conference attendees on how to mean what you say without saying what you mean.

Living Barclay. Dean Freiday several years ago performed a wonderful service for Friends by editing *Barclay's Apology in Modern English.* The volume's only major shortcoming is that it still requires careful reading and thoughtfulness. For those who don't have the time or desire to study their faith, *Living Barclay* is the perfect solution. More a patchwork than a paraphrase, it gathers in a single collection the principal Quaker slogans and clichés of thought. To each is added a sentence, or for the more difficult concepts, a paragraph of explanation. The pithy sentence summaries on "sacrament," "the Word," and "that of God" are especially catchy and memorable.

Other titles include *A User's Guide to Pastors and Meeting Secretaries* and *Doubling Your Attendance in Six Months.*

In addition to books, POF Press is offering a variety of other products including postcards, stationery, posters, buttons, and items distinctly designed for our technological era. POF plans to introduce Friendly User computer software (user friendly, of course) and home video games. "Underground Railroad" is praised for its "livid, vivid black-and-white images" and said to be more fun than "Donkey Kong" or "Frogger." The audio- and video-cassette tapes of unprogrammed meetings have been an early, but quiet success.

The purpose of POF Press is to offer a wide range of radically contemporary, easy-to-use products for the modern Quaker on the go. POF has responded directly to market research which advises that only the spiritual elite and religious overachievers read books on prayer, doctrine, significant contemporary issues, or even good biography. It has targeted instead the great mass of people who need to fit religion in at the edges of busy lives. "How-to" books, light biography (for example, *Quaker Quarterback*), and similar titles will dominate their catalog.

For more information (prospective authors please query before sending manuscripts), write: Publishers of Fluff and Other Stuff, Dept. RJF, 2100 University Avenue, Wichita, KS 67213. ☺

Thomas Kelly: An Appreciation

This month is the fortieth January since Thomas Kelly passed away suddenly on January 17, 1941. By biblical timekeeping, these forty years would mark a generation since Tom Kelly spoke and wrote among Friends.

Though the generation just past has not known Kelly in person, many thousands of them have been drawn to him through the writings of his last few years. The steady success of *A Testament of Devotion* for over forty years witnesses to his importance to Friends and many other Christians.

I write more as a debtor than a critic. I can only be thankful that his heart and mind saw deeply and that he could describe what he saw. Passages from Kelly, now familiar friends, still stir me as if they were new. As I pass on to my students this legacy, which my teachers gave me, I see renewed resolve and challenges in them as well.

What is it Kelly saw that makes his writing so enduring? Several ideas stand out. For example, he discovered for himself that complete devotion to God opens a world of delight and freedom that the self-centered cannot even imagine. In that discovery he also saw the futility of half-hearted, "sensible" devotion. He wrote, for example, in "Hasten unto God:"

> "This may sound platitudinous. But it is preached all too little. The center of religion is in a living, vital, unspeakably intimate fellowship of the soul with God, wherein we sing and dance and leap for joy in His Presence. And some of us have found that life, that overturning, realigning experience of Him in His immediacy, and we walk in joy and power. But some have, I fear, never even guessed that there is possible such a life with God as makes all creation new—although the words

have fallen on our ears since childhood. Even the Quaker preaching upon the *immediacy,* of Divine Presence, for which there is no substitute in religious learnedness or endeavor, even this preaching has been a thing for many Quakers to *believe in*, not a gateway into the experience of God Himself. I say this pointedly and without apology. For if we knew Him and His Power and Glory in full immediacy and walked daily in humility and erectness of soul and such resplendent gleams of divine light and glory would shine out from us as would kindle other lives into a heavenly flame, and we should shake the countryside for ten miles around. . . . Hasten unto God. Why? Not because we ought to. Fellowship with God isn't a bitter duty. Fellowship with God is the deepest joy of human existence." (*The Eternal Promise*, p. 71)

Like a prophet who had seen God and could then declare the truth, Kelly shared his vision of God. This vision would not accept "mediocrity" in religious devotion, nor would it accommodate religiosity that failed to touch all of life. Devotion to God penetrates every corner of life, every scrap of time, every act. Prayer and service share a common root. So Kelly wrote, "The straightest road to the social gospel runs through profound mystical experience." (*The Eternal Promise*, p. 3)

Although Thomas Kelly was not narrowly sectarian, he was thoroughly a Quaker. He longed for Friends to "have a vivid sense of the *freshness* and the *newness* of the Quaker discovery and emphasis." I suspect that if Friends together could discover for themselves what Tom Kelly saw, we would know a new day of joy and power which would restore us to one another, to God, and to useful service in our world.

In the meanwhile, I am glad that Thomas Kelly, though now a generation gone, still stands to point the way.

[Almost all of Kelly's published work is still available: *A Testament of Devotion*, Harper and Row; *The Eternal Promise*, Friends United Press; and *The Reality of the Spiritual World*, Pendle Hill Pamphlets. Order through Quaker Hill Bookstore.]

Words, Words, WORDS!!

The woodcut image of a preacher seen now years ago still burns itself into my memory. In brown monochrome the preacher stands with crooked finger raised, neck thrust forward, hinged by a stiff clerical collar to his angular torso. Face drawn, head balding, eyes vacant, his open mouth is filled with words—"WORDS" tumbling out in blocky wood grain. "WORDS, WORDS, WORDS" stacked up on one another, jostling each other for space like children in lunch line or matrons surging to snatch prized sale goods in Filene's Bargain Basement. WORDS. But these are not words like the Lord jammed into the mouth of a reluctant Jeremiah, words that have power to tear up and to destroy, to build and to plant, words of life, words of God. Instead, these are dead words, manufactured words, chunks of mass production words to be hammered together into proper sermons, correct public prayers, and religious talk apparently knowing and profound, though merely multisyllabic froth. These are words of those who "do not possess what they profess."

Any who have encountered God deeply feel the presumption of trying to describe that reality in words, though they must. Yet, even allowing for that risk, how dreadful to think that my words about God and life might be lifeless chunks of rhetoric cluttering the pathway for others. How humbling to know that at times they have been like that. How much I long instead to see my mouth open with pictures flowing out. Not flat pictures in cartoon speech balloons, but 3-D pictures, living pictures which burst their way through balloon boundaries as surely as the grass reclaims abandoned sidewalks, slipping through their seams, cracking their apparently impenetrable surfaces.

When I dare to open my mouth about God I want life to flow out—life given, life cherished, life lived full, the life of God within me. No "mere words" will do.

Words—too often prisons, false security, the mask of ignorance. How wise that God chose to break through syntax and lexicon with life. "The Word was made flesh and dwelt among us, and we beheld his glory . . . full of grace and truth. (John 1:14 KJ) The Word still seeks to break through blindness, hard hearts, and crusty tradition to be enfleshed in our words and in our living, so that these can bear and be life rather than merely wooden signposts on a way forgotten.

In *The Sacrament of the Present Moment*, de Caussade speaks eloquently of this life:

> "And if souls knew how to unite themselves to [God's loving] purpose, their lives would be a succession of divine scriptures, continuing to the end of time, not written with ink on paper, but on each human heart. . . . And so the sequel to the New Testament is being written now, by action and suffering. Saintly souls are in the succession of the prophets and the Apostles, not by writing canonical books, but by continuing the history of divine purpose with their lives, whose moments are so many syllables and sentences through which it is vividly expressed. The books the Holy Spirit is writing are living, and every soul a volume in which the divine author makes a true revelation of his word, explaining it to every heart, unfolding it in every moment." (pp. 73–74)

As remarkable as it may seem, our lives can witness to and reflect the very character and glory of God. So may our words be living, and may our living be, in some tangible though mysterious way, God's word.

The Tide of Light

I sat stunned with dread and fear, struggling for belief. It was a night when the ocean of darkness roared at violent high tide, spitting defiantly, threatening everything in its path.

The tide began to roll in with an old movie on TV, a story of three kidnappers and of the man and woman they capture. The sense of evil crescendos throughout. Violence and fear are its basic theme through which are woven the sneering abuse of power, the demeaning of the simplest human acts and emotions, uproarious delight in others' terror, sexual abuse. The story climaxes as the kidnappers free their victims in the wilderness, only to hunt them like animals. It plays to a bloody end without even a slender thread of good to grasp after. Kidnappers and kidnapped alike act wickedly. Even the vigilant huntsman who concludes the movie is evil. The darkness seemed so strong.

But there was more. Even as the evil tide washed over me I could see that the movie mirrored a larger picture. Politicians, smiling amiably, promising to increase our ability to blow up the world. Scientists cleverly calculating how to do it most efficiently, plotting missile routes and kill ratios. Pimps, hookers, johns—all perpetrators and victims. Parents ignoring or beating children. Children despising their parents with screams and with vicious silence. Lovers using and discarding one another. Those whose hunt for the good life makes people their quarry. TV preachers hawking a red-white-and-blue plastic Jesus. Cheats. Ax-murderers. Slum landlords. The Klan. Addicts to violence. Hypocrites. Oppressors of the poor. Self-appointed gods in self-made universes. A catalog of rebels.

It recalls the world before the Flood, a world "filled with violence." No one could justly find fault if God would again regret having made people.

The surge of dark waters washed away any sentimental temptation to think that everything is basically all right—that all this world needs is a few goodhearted folk to make some minor adjustments. We too easily underestimate the severity and pervasiveness of evil in the world, yet we are caught in its web. Apathy toward evil, participation (directly or indirectly) in it, or personal initiation of it implicates everyone. Reality (and the Gospel) refute wishful thinking about the essential goodness of society and its people. Beach buckets full of naïve optimism will not turn back this angry tide. Evil threatens to capture us all in its undertow.

Can it be possible that an ocean of light will overcome this ocean of darkness? Can God still act in power? Or are things completely beyond control?

Ancient Israel's doubts in distress remind us of our own. Perhaps God is no longer powerful. (Psalm 77:10) Perhaps the Lord doesn't know our troubles or care about them. (Isaiah 40:27) In their despair the Hebrews answered that God will prevail. God, who first rebuked darkness by saying, "Let there be light," who first put the chaotic waters in their place, who created the world to be good and is transforming it to be good again. God, neither weakened nor weary, will prevail.

In an equally dark time, George Fox saw the ocean of light overflowing the ocean of darkness. Sustained in part by this vision, Fox lived boldly, "trampling evil underfoot."

If we underestimate the severity of evil, we also overestimate its power. Evil is not the only word. Evil will not be the last word. In this season we recall the story of a star that stood over a stable. Probably few noticed the star. Even fewer noticed the baby born there. Among the government bureaucrats, the soldiers, the harried innkeepers, and the tired travelers, who would notice? Yet, improbable as it seems, the Light, incarnate in a Jewish baby boy, shone. That birth and life, that death and new life, still shine as a witness that God has not given up on a darkened world.

In the New Testament vision of the new heaven and new earth, the threatening, chaotic sea has disappeared (Revelation 21:23–25) and Christ the Lamb shines so brightly that night is left with not even a shadow. (Revelation 21:23–25)

With evil so starkly real, I can barely understand how light can be the end rather than darkness, or why God should even care to make it so. I sing with more bravery than bravado, "Though the wrong seems oft so strong, God is the Ruler yet." Yet perhaps it is the essence of faith that, even though we struggle, we believe.

The ocean of light is overcoming. . . .

Remembering Bethlehem

I blushed, then smiled, to have stumbled onto Christmas in the Church of the Nativity in Bethlehem. I had entered merely as a Sunday tourist when I heard the Roman Catholic congregation in the left chapel celebrating the twelfth day of Christmas. In the worship space straight ahead the little Armenian Orthodox congregation was observing their Christmas Day. Clumsy tourism aside, I was moved to arrive on this day where Christians have celebrated Christmas in a church on this site for 1700 years.

What I discovered down in the Grotto of the Nativity, the stable-cave below the church, at first rattled my Quaker sensibilities. But take away the abundant candles, the lamps, the decorative hangings and the marble floor with its 14-point silver star marking the very spot of Jesus' birth, the cave seemed pretty plain. As a German family knelt a few steps away at the Chapel of the Manger and sang "Stille Nacht," I thought, "If not here, probably like here." Hidden, barren. Who would even notice? It's hard to imagine still that shepherds would hurry to this place and beam with hopes of peace and joy when they discovered a newborn baby.

Cards and songs aside, the Bethlehem they hurried to was not serene and still. It was bustling and bursting at the seams, full of visitors grumbling at the census and Caesar's taxes. The soldiers guaranteeing the "peace of Rome" controlled the crowds and counted heads. They had compelled many Josephs and maybe other too-pregnant Marys to return to their ancestral home to get on the tax rolls, whether or not they knew a cousin with a sleeper sofa.

Occupiers and rebels have often fought over this place. Bethlehem's first Church of the Nativity was burned down in a rebellion after 200 years, and the one now standing has an odd, centuries-old entrance first designed to keep Ottoman horsemen out of the church. Even today concrete walls, fences, and trenches surround and squeeze this little town whose "peace" the occupying armies guarantee with tanks, F-16 fighter jets and Apache helicopters.

Yet it is in bloody, troubled, turbulent Bethlehem that God acts, that God announces joy and peace. Bethlehem native and local Lutheran pastor Mitri Raheb writes:

> "Christians have to take Christmas in Bethlehem seriously, because on that holy night and in this very place, God chose to be very concrete, to take flesh, and to take our world very seriously. We Christians [in Bethlehem] are unafraid to face the brutal reality around us because we believe in a power mightier than walls and put our faith in a peace that exceeds all human understanding." (*Bethlehem Besieged*, pp. 144–145)

Since I know that our brothers and sisters in Bethlehem steadily suffer violence and oppression, Raheb's bold words encourage me. So do George Fox' words to Friends enduring harassment and imprisonment: "Sing and rejoice, ye children of the Day and of the Light; for the Lord is at work in this thick night of darkness that may be felt. …the Lamb shall have victory over them all." (Epistle 227)

Yet some days it's hard to sustain hope when the rising tide of evil crashes in and is even blessed in God's name. People of faith have long, and rightly, struggled over this. In such times the Bible's complaint psalms help give us voice: "Why? How long? When will you do something, God?" But these psalms, too, even in the darkest times, remind us that God does act, that God will prevail.

In Bethlehem, with its obscurity and with its cast of unlikely heroes, God acted decisively. It surprised the shepherds; it scared Herod. It brings us hope, a hope in which to anchor, a hope in which to act. As Raheb points out, it is not enough to be "joyful peace talkers rather than blessed peacemakers." The baby born in Bethlehem calls us all to live joyfully and boldly in the power of the Lord that is over all.

Maybe God's Laughing

Positively perplexed, to put it politely. As I write we're about a week away from the war of aggression George W. Bush is so eager to start. Unless Saddam sends him the keys to Iraqi palaces and goes into exile somewhere (the checkstand news rags say in New Jersey!). Frankly I'm angry and disgusted at the lies, the fear-mongering, the bullying and buying of allies, the siren song of war. By now you'll know what happened. But for now I am, not really so politely, perplexed.

I wonder, though, whether God might be laughing. In the Bible superpowers and their arrogant leaders often get comic treatment, not for clowning or clever puns, but for the comedy of the absurd, of pretentiousness, of ambitions and egos run amuck. Psalm 2 warns that God "who sits in the heavens laughs" at rulers and nations who would rival God's purpose and power. As dangerous as they are, they look so silly.

Humorous stories offer the warning, too. Nebuchadnezzar, for example, the powerful Babylonian king who destroyed Jerusalem, literally gets turned out to pasture to eat like an ox. (Daniel 4) King Belshazzar, his son, hosting a lavish state party inside beautiful and secure Babylon, saw fingers of a human hand writing on the palace wall. White as a ghost and scared out of his wits, he yelled for his advisors, all the while his knees knocked together and his legs went limp (or, as one suggests, the unlocking of his loins might have had a moister outcome). (Daniel 5)

In a satire song, another, unnamed King of Babylon finally dies, only to be greeted by the kings he has cruelly dispatched to Sheol before him, all the while he bragged, "I will rival the Most High." The grinning kings' welcome speech includes, "So you too have been brought to nothing, like ourselves . . . underneath you a bed of maggots and over you a blanket of worms." (Isaiah 14:3–21 JB)

Egypt and Edom were legendary for their wisdom, but the prophets needled their kings' best and brightest advisers. Isaiah says Egypt's wisest counselors are stupid and that God will so confuse them and confound their plans that they'll look like drunks staggering around in vomit. (Isaiah 19: 3,11,14) Jeremiah wonders whether there's any wisdom left in Edom since the smartest ones seem to have run out of common sense and clutch only to wisdom gone stale. (Jeremiah 49: 7) Prideful people of power don't much like (or even get) humor directed at them, but the people marked with the kings' bootprints on their backs no doubt giggled and guffawed in truth and pain.

Not all the Bible's warnings against arrogant power are framed with humor, whether they're directed to prideful Israel and Judah or to their neighbors. The message is clear: ultimately God rules and nobody is out of God's reach, not even super-duper powers and their leaders. Indeed, God topples the powerful and raises up the weak. Pharaoh couldn't keep the Hebrews captive. Massively walled Babylon was overthrown in a night. Unrivalled Nineveh collapsed to the applause and cheers of those who had suffered her cruelties.

In troubling times like these I take comfort, even confidence, in knowing that God is in charge and will prevail. But, like Habakkuk, I'm not sure that God will choose to solve the problem in the way I think best. Based on the biblical record, I'm sure that, even when they're given a divine mandate, God will bring down arrogant powerbrokers and strutting thugs, in God's wisdom, time, and way. But I'm not so sure that this is good news if my nation's leaders are among the proud bullies and when lots of people around me are thumping their chests in approval.

Maybe you have to be a little careful about when you pray "Thy Kingdom come, Thy will be done on earth . . ." But it has come and it will. I think I need to join Habakkuk, perplexed and faithful. Even if everything falls apart, he said, "Yet I will rejoice in the Lord . . . who is my strength; he makes my feet like the feet of a deer, and enables me to go on the heights." (Habakkuk 3:18–19 NIV)

Immanuel

Recently Friends University's Drama Department presented a very moving production of Dorothy Sayer's play, *The Man Born To Be King*. The audience was quickly drawn into the life of Jesus, gentle, full of humor, proclaiming Truth, intensely devoted to God. We grinned with those who were healed, marveled as we shared bread multiplied to feed the multitudes, and knew for ourselves the wonder-filled bewilderment of the disciples as this glorious life played itself toward tragedy. The pain of the crucifixion appalled us. Its love reached us. Resurrection brought hope.

This experience instantly joined itself to those moments in life that will never be forgotten. Somehow the familiar story had come more intensely alive. Then the lights came up, the curtain closed, and the audience filed out. Some moved silently, obviously still gripped by what they had just experienced. Others chattered their way out, evaluating actors, gossiping about family and friends. They hurried on to parties, to homework, to romance, even perhaps to prayer.

I stayed on for a while in the auditorium while the stage crew and the cast began to dismantle the set. Within an hour the forms that had been hills and houses, courtyards, boats, and tombs would be gone, leaving the stage barren and stark. Melancholy questions came to me: Is it back to business as usual now? Or has it become merely a familiar story which, each time it treads the path of our hearts, packs down the soil even harder, so that good seed cannot take root on its thick crusty surface? After the lights come up and the set is struck, is the story's chief actor still with us?

We might easily long for the glory of yesterdays to burst through gloomy todays. How we would have thrilled to be among the five thousand eating multiplied bread or later in the company of the disciples at prayer when the Holy Spirit fell on them.

We might just as quickly long to see the glory that will brighten some future, to "go on to glory," to join in the final triumph of God, or, less otherworldly, to come to some dramatic and unusual point in our spiritual growth.

Yet, for all our longing, the glory surrounding us and confronting us in each day may completely escape our notice. We too easily fail to see Immanuel, God-with-us. God's power still triumphs for us in each day's living. The Life-giver still multiplies loaves to feed us and touches broken spirits and bodies to heal us. The Divine Love still reaches us, directly and through the incredible gift of love poured out in friendship. The glorious creation constantly whispers and shouts among its parts, "God-with-us!"

If this is true, if Christ, who said, "I am with you always," is right, then we have wonderful news. The one in whom we have seen God's glory is still with us, and in that Powerful Presence is all that we need for joy, liberty, and wholeness. The Christ of glory remains among us, not relaxing backstage in a dressing room or removed from reality once the make-up has been wiped away.

Our central witness has been that Christ is present in power. When the stage has been struck, the mangers folded, the angel wings crumpled and tucked away for another year, let's remember that the Light still shines and lives among us, bringing glory and hope.

Study **Guide**

The following study guide suggests some ways this book might be used for group study and discussion or even for personal study. It distributes the essays among fourteen topical groupings and suggests questions that may respond to and/or build on the readings. Certainly there might be other questions and other approaches, such as reading and discussing one or two of the essays at a time in a more focused way. Explore and enjoy!

1. Being Friends

Suggested Readings:

Walking Cheerfully
Children of Light
Quaker Mush
Convinced and Convincing
Ordinary People
Family Resemblance

Reflection Questions:

1. One way to dismiss heroes of the faith is to call them "saints." In praising them we can also make them irrelevant, making them very unlike ourselves. What can we do, instead, to let extraordinary lives guide and encourage our own living? How can we imagine God at work through ordinary people?

2. What practical steps might we take to become both "convinced" and "convincing?"

3. What are some of the most important ways that modern Friends can show "family resemblance?"

4. "Walking cheerfully" in response to God's initiative in people's lives suggests a joyful presence. How can we speak and act to make following Christ seem like "good news?"

2. Resources for Living

Suggested Readings:

Reckless Abandon
Molded by Scripture
Above All, Prayer
Checklists for Extraordinary Ordinary Living
Tasty Torah

Reflection Questions:

1. In what ways does "reckless abandon" become necessary for living effectively as Christ's people? What can hinder such recklessness?

2. What are some of the ways in which you have found great delight in or have been shaped deeply by Scripture? What are some practical ways of nurturing such experiences?

3. What are some of the challenges to having prayer become a steady, core practice in our lives? What might we do to overcome them?

4. What practices in using the "queries" have you found particularly helpful? Which of the ideas in "Checklists . . ." do you think you/we might usefully try?

3. Sacramental Living

Suggested Readings:

Sanctuary
Sacramental Breakdown
The Binoculared Ones
Immanuel

Reflection Questions:

1. What experiences can you recall when you unexpectedly became aware of Christ's presence?

2. What active steps can we take to keep us alert to Christ steadily among us?

3. In Isaiah 7 where we read the promise of a child named "Immanuel," King Ahaz of Judah was threatened by his intent-on-war neighbors Israel and Syria, and he was taking conventional steps to meet that threat. In what ways in our ordinary experience are we tempted to take conventional steps rather than rely on God-with-us?

4. In what ways, like the "binoculared ones," can we experience the world in ways that remind us that God is with us?

4. Living Day to Day

Suggested Readings:

The Tyranny of the Good
The Frantic Pace
Shall Pac-Man Be Praised?
Glad for Today
Watching Our Lips Move

Reflection Questions:

1. What things divert us from living gladly in the present? What about the message of Ecclesiastes might remind us of the value of living gladly today?

2. Many of us are caught up in busy, stressful lives. Do you think this is from external or internal pressures? What practical steps or perspectives can help us choose greater wholeness?

3. What principles do you think should guide our choices about recreation and use of discretionary time? How can we be joyful and thoughtful, not grim, in making these choices?

4. When is it most difficult to control how we speak? What steps can we take to let our words and the whisperings of our hearts (Psalm 19:14) be acceptable to God?

5. Practical Principles

Suggested Readings:

The Honest Truth
The Rev. Dr. George Fox
Fixing Education
Light for Learning
Thomas Kelly: An Appreciation
Words, Words, WORDS!!

Reflection Questions:

1. Over time Friends have practiced specific "distinctives" or "testimonies" as a way of living transformed lives, where words and behavior correspond. Among the "distinctives" you know about, which ones seem to be particularly relevant today?

2. What are some of the sharpest challenges to keep integrity in our ordinary experience? Why are these particularly tempting? What steps can we take to nurture and guard integrity?

3. The early Quakers refusal to tip hats and use "honorific titles" grew out of their commitment to show true respect to everyone. In what ways might we show false respect today? What active steps can we take to show genuine respect for everyone? Who don't you want to include in "everyone?" Who do you especially want to think that you really respect them? Why?

4. What did you find especially engaging the reflection on Kelly? If you know Kelly, what other themes or phrases do you find helpful?

5. Friends have been pioneers in education in many ways. In what ways do you think Friends can continue to provide valuable insight and support in both public and private schools?

6. Simplifying Simplicity

Suggested Readings:

Hearing Voices
The All-Rounder

Reflection Questions:

1. Many people understand simplicity as dealing mostly with money and possessions. How might that change if we were to make John Woolman's choice to pay "steady attention to the voice of the True Shepherd" the central guide to simplicity?

2. Some teach about simplicity that outward practices grow out of inward transformation. Others teach that outward practices can bring inner transformation. In what ways is each of these approaches helpful?

3. In what ways does our daily experience challenge the desire to live in simplicity?

4. Some who practice simplicity witness to it being a way of freedom and joy rather than cramped constraint and deprivation. Why do you think they say this?

7. The Life of Worship

Suggested Readings:

The Performance
Prepare for Worship
Stopwatch Silence
Is Preaching Okay?

Reflection Questions:

1. In a "gathered meeting" we feel that together we have genuinely encountered God. What are your most memorable experiences of a "gathered meeting?" Try to identify what made it so.

2. What are some of the specific ways we can prepare for and strengthen the meeting for worship? What is the importance of seeing this as everyone's responsibility?

3. Of your pet peeves about worship (most people have some), which of them are merely petty and personal and which may suggest positive ways to strengthen the life of worship?

4. How can a meeting honor and encourage vital vocal ministry, whether from appointed speakers or others?

8. Nurturing Ministry

Suggested Readings:

Fit for Ministry
What Do You Know by Heart?
A Case (Cassette?) for Recording
Nothing Against Women, But . . .
The Abraham Farrington Society

Reflection Questions:

1. In what ways can we actually release and encourage individuals in their use of gifts in public ministry?

2. In what ways does your meeting actively look for emerging gifts in ministry and seek ways to nurture their growth?

3. In what ways does the author's description of "recording" in public ministry contrast with or complement your understanding? How might this view shape a meeting's understanding of when to recommend someone for recording?

4. What active steps could Friends take to develop the emerging gifts of inexperienced ministers?

9. Meetings that Matter

Suggested Readings:

The Nonsense of the Meeting
More Nonsense
The Threshing Meeting
The Meeting for Clearness
The Meeting for Learning

Reflection Questions:

1. Without getting nasty now, name an especially memorable example of nonsense in a meeting for business, whether through manipulation, distrust or ordinary human stupidity.

2. What positive steps can we take to make decisions effectively under Christ's guidance?

3. If you can, share a positive experience of a meeting for clearness or, without that name, of seeking the help of people with spiritual discernment.

4. The "threshing meeting" of early Friends often involved street preaching, large crowds in open fields or a crowd crammed into a rented English pub. Brainstorm what venues today might offer a chance to encounter "seekers."

5. How might we heighten the value of the "meeting for learning," especially for adults?

10. Embracing Leadership

Suggested Readings:

Elders as Movers and Shakers (or Is That Quakers?)
Elders and Schizophrenia
Praying for Leaders

Reflection Questions:

1. What are some ways we can assist and encourage elders and other leaders in our meetings?

2. One of the readings suggests that the word "elder" leads a double life. What steps can elders and others take to make the verb "to elder" a positive word about guidance, care and encouragement?

3. Sometimes elders are viewed as people who protect what is, who just guard the past. How can we help elders become a group that holds our core values and, at the same time, leads with vision and initiative toward the future?

4. Which leaders specifically should we hold in our prayers? What should we pray on their behalf? How might we assure that such prayer is happening?

11. Living Well Together

Suggested Readings:

Treasuring One Another
In the Care of the Meeting
Instead of Hating Weddings
On Being Noticeably Good
The Timid Sixty
Deadheads and Fanatics
Hospitable Friends

Reflection Questions:

1. Many people long for significant community, partly because it's so hard to experience in an extremely privatistic culture. How can individuals take the initiative to steadily be a part of the church community? How can the meeting act to welcome and nurture individuals? How do we move toward mutual trust?

2. The New Testament vision of the Church is of a people built together which transcends ethnicity, gender, social class and all other ways we normally divide into groups. What steps can we take to treasure one another genuinely beyond all normal boundaries?

3. Brainstorm ideas about how we might stir up hospitality in our life together.

4. What barriers and attractions are there in entrusting ourselves to "the care of the meeting?" How can we make that an inviting reality?

12. Joy in Justice and Mercy

Suggested Readings:

Beds of Ease
Good News and Peace
Anointed or Just Greasy?
Prophets for Dummies

Reflection Questions:

1. Historically Friends have naturally connected service and compassion to genuine discipleship. How is it that "justice and mercy" grow naturally out of "walking humbly with God?"

2. As we continue to declare the "good news of peace," what might be some practical ways both to call people to be reconciled and to teach them to become reconcilers?

3. The Bible often tells us that God loves the world more than we can imagine and shows special care for the oppressed, the poor and the vulnerable. God's love will bring deliverance and justice. How does knowing this guide our action and give us hope?

4. What specific needs for justice and mercy might guide our meeting's ministry in our own community?

13. Light-Hearted News

Suggested Readings:

Stand-Up Jesus
St. Fool
Publishers of Fluff and Other Stuff
(Walking Cheerfully)

Reflection Questions:

1. Why is the man on the Quaker Oats box smiling? How representative is he of normal Quakers or was he borrowed from a Lutheran Oats box?

2. How is it possible to be funny and serious at the same time? In what ways can you imagine Jesus doing this? In what ways can you imagine you doing this?

3. Some suggest that at its core the Gospel is comedy. Surprising, unexpected things happen—the hopeless outclassed folks win; the too-good-to-be-true becomes true; and, as with Abraham and Sarah, the nothing's-too-difficult-for-God erupts in great laughter. How does Paul continue that theme? How does that invite us into light-hearted discipleship?

4. "Publishers of Fluff . . ." barely begins to fill out its full catalog potential. What suggestions do you have for other lightweight titles? The backhand of the essay also suggests that folks need to feed on more than froth. What kinds of resources would you recommend?

14. The Ocean of Light

Suggested Readings:

The Healing Light
The Heavens Are Falling
The Tide of Light
Remembering Bethlehem
Maybe God's Laughing

Reflection Questions:

1. How readily are you able to live in the confidence that "the power of the Lord is over all?" When you're able to do that, how does it affect your living?

2. What are the occasions that the "ocean of darkness" seems particularly vivid or powerful to you? What's the chance that you're giving darkness too much credit?

3. In what ways may we collaborate in God's work, letting our light penetrate the darkness, convinced that God is prevailing?

4. Given the circumstances of your life and culture, why might it be both good news and bad news for you if God were to act powerfully against the darkness you see?

5. How can we come to a place of confidence and rest as in Psalm 46, "Be still and know that I am God" (KJ) and Habakkuk 3, even if everything falls apart, "I will rejoice in . . . God my Savior?" (v. 18 NIV)

CPSIA information can be obtained
at www.ICGtesting.com
Printed in the USA
LVOW11s1548030618
579410LV00001B/5/P